RAISING CAPITAL

CAPITAL

—— for ——

REAL ESTATE

How to Establish Credibility,
Attract Investors, and Fund Deals

HUNTER THOMPSON

Dedication

To my beautiful wife Chrissy,
who is the love of my life.

To my mother Juliet,
who has encouraged me to pursue
each of my interests intensely.

And to the Asym Capital investors and the
Cash Flow Connections Real Estate Podcast listeners,
who have made all of this possible.

Table of Contents

A Timeless Playbook for Raising Capital in Today's Environment

by Ryan Smith

Since the formation of our first fund nearly a decade ago, I have witnessed a significant shift in the way real estate deals are capitalized.

Over the last few years, a combination of technology and regulatory changes, coupled with the growing belief that investors can adequately manage their own investments, has fueled the rise in popularity of investing in syndications. While not without its risks, this pursuit has allowed many investors to implement a passive approach to investing in real estate, as an increasing number of investors seek diversification outside of the more traditional ways to allocate their capital.

As the market for these investments has grown, investors have turned to the internet to source potential operators with whom they can invest. For syndicators, this can provide both a cost-effective and scalable way to access capital.

Today, many investors hold what could be deemed a traditional portfolio composed of an allocation of stocks, bonds, and mutual funds. Over the past several years, we have seen an increase in demand for alternative assets among investors. We expect this to continue for the foreseeable future.

This book is the first of its kind to break down the systems and processes that are working for many of real estate's industry leaders in the non-institutional space, people who have created reliable methods to provide themselves with capital when it is time to close a deal in today's climate.

In *Raising Capital for Real Estate*, Hunter synthesizes helpful and repeatable methods he has both learned and created, providing you with not only a clear understanding of what to do and how to do it, but also endless details, nuances, and specifics that could easily take years to uncover without this book's guidance.

This book will likely save you a great deal of time in putting together a clear plan, but in the end, there is no substitute for hard work. Implementing the tools outlined in these pages will take time, determination, and perseverance, but the payoff for those who are motivated can be substantial.

While Hunter does provide an updated look at real estate–focused education, resources, apps, and strategies, the underlying themes of the book will provide you with a sturdy foundation on which to build a successful real estate firm that can last well into the future. The book combines many "new-school" strategies while still placing the focus on people and valuing relationships.

One section of the book that really resonated with me was Hunter's discussion about identifying and attracting mentors.

I myself have been very fortunate to be able to stand on the shoulders of giants—the numerous men and women who have helped me tremendously through my life. As it has been said, "Water joins a moving stream." The currency for these relationships is humility: humbly given and humbly received. Many individuals, knowingly and unknowingly, have contributed a great deal to me. I'd like to share one story with you, as it sets the stage for anyone who is looking for a quantum leap in their pursuits.

SEEING THROUGH THE FOG

After college, I found myself with a small base of capital, good credit, and an awareness of what building a real estate business could afford, namely: periodic income, capital appreciation (equity), and tax benefits. Accordingly, my wife Jamie and I began building our portfolio, which started with single-family residential properties and raw land. Soon thereafter, we graduated to manufactured housing communities. Little did we know, a chance encounter was soon going to dramatically accelerate our path to success.

Around 2005, I had been asked to give a talk in Boston on investing in real estate. At the conference, a gentleman approached me, and we began talking. I was in my mid-20s and he was 30 years my senior. Without going into too much detail, I found both him and his accomplishments beyond impressive. In the months and years after the conference, we stayed in touch by phone and in-person meetings.

During one of our conversations, he mentioned that he wanted to introduce me to a friend of his. His friend, it turns out, began investing in real estate in the '70s and, at one point, had owned and or operated more than 40,000 self-storage units. I could barely wrap my head around that number, much less that I was being asked if I wanted to meet with this gentleman.

I told my friend that I would be willing to walk across country backwards for the opportunity—and I meant it. One night, a few weeks later, my friend called me and said that the self-storage operator would be willing to meet me the following day in Newport Beach, California. That was great, but I was on the other side of the country in Orlando, Florida (not enough time to walk backwards!). Regardless, I told him I would be there. His parting words were, "Do not be late."

The next morning, my wife Jamie and I flew across the country, landed at LAX, changed in the airport restroom, and drove to Newport Beach to have dinner with my friend and the gentleman he wanted to introduce us to. The man was Brian Dahn, one of the largest self-storage owners in the United States. Despite many obstacles, we were early.

During dinner, Brian proceeded to ask Jamie and me numerous questions about our background and our experience in real estate. On the surface, it could have felt like he was trying to size up our business credentials, but now knowing Brian the way I do, he was really looking for the intangibles. What inspired us? Through what lens did we view the world? What kind of people were we? These were the questions he was contemplating.

Thankfully, our responses resonated with him, and he began to open up. That night, he shared with us countless gifts of knowledge that still impact my thinking about the business today, but none more powerful than the concept of the Reg D 506(b) offering, which could allow us to pool investor capital and, therefore, scale our real estate business over time. This was the first time I had ever heard of the concept, but I instantly saw the potential.

Today, you will find that we have an image of a train track going far into the distance on many of our marketing materials. The reason I selected this image is related to this story.

Before this dinner, I believed that I was on the right track, but it was as if the path was covered in dense fog. I could see the tracks laid out just before me but not much further. After dinner, it was as if the fog had been blown away, the sun was shining, and I could see 100 miles ahead. I knew I was on the right track, now I just needed to move, which has never been my struggle.

Shortly after that meeting in 2010, we launched our first fund, which required $2,000,000 in equity.

As daunting of a task as it seemed, the process of raising our first fund began with Jamie and me sitting at the dining room table with our cell phones in hand and literally calling our contacts in alphabetical order, starting with A and working our way towards Z.

Unbelievably, we were able to raise the $2,000,000 in a few short months. To this day, raising our first fund is something that I am incredibly proud of, and I am grateful to each investor who took a chance.

Today, we, through various entities, are one of the larger mobile home park owners in the U.S. We have opened seven funds with plans to open others in the future. Through these affiliated entities, we have acquired more than $500,000,000 worth of real estate in approximately 30 states in the U.S. Our business has grown into one that involves big numbers, but big things start with small beginnings. If you are reading this book, I would imagine that the seed of something big may have already begun to sprout.

Operating in this space has been incredibly rewarding, but the aspect I value the most is the relationships we've built over the years. Those include everyone we are privileged to serve—our residents, our customers, our investors, our team members—and those with whom we have strategic partnerships; one of whom being Hunter Thompson.

Many of you reading this book may have a solid idea of the direction you are heading, but you may not clearly see the tracks leading you there. You may feel like you are on the brink of something special but are unsure of the challenges you may face just around the bend. This lack of clarity may rightfully cause you to hesitate to move quickly, knowing that traveling without a clear line of sight can be inefficient at best and disastrous at worst.

My hope for you is that this book will allow you dissipate the fog that stands in your way and that the content in these pages will reveal the tracks that lead you to your goals, so that you can travel safely, confidently, and expediently on your amazing real estate journey.

All aboard!

Ryan Smith,
Principal of Elevation Capital Group

CHAPTER 1

Europe Caught My Portfolio on Fire

2008 was an all-out nightmare for many people in the United States. Skyrocketing unemployment rates, government bail-outs, historically sound businesses shutting their doors—and, of course, extensive real estate foreclosures—dominated the media. Around every corner, you'd see foreclosure signs alongside vacant apartments advertising "Free Rent for Two Months, Plus a 52" Plasma TV." Even those who were originally optimistic lost confidence in the economy as the truth gradually sank in: This was not just another recession, and the return to normal might take years longer than anticipated.

Luckily, I was a college student at the time and, as a result, mostly insulated from the turmoil. Yes, it was clear that the economy was struggling, but my college life remained virtually unchanged: go to class, come home, watch *The Wire*, eat ramen noodles, repeat.

I didn't know much about investing, but the one mantra I heard many times was "buy when blood is in the streets." Even with my limited knowledge, I knew the Great Recession was exactly the type of economic condition that phrase referred to.

I'd always had an affinity for economics, but the aftermath of the 2008 market crash became the catalyst for an intense obsession with learning as much as I could about finance, investing, and market cycles. I didn't want to leave a single stone unturned. Since the stock market was the most popular and easily accessible way to invest, it ended up being the first investment vehicle that attracted me.

I studied the greats like Warren Buffet and Charlie Munger, read books on value investing and day trading, and eventually started investing proceeds from previous entrepreneurial endeavors (including a stint as a professional poker player) in companies I thought would be well-positioned once the economy got back on its feet, as I anticipated it would.

As with pretty much anyone who started investing in stocks in 2008, the early results were pretty spectacular. Luckily, some bullish investments in Apple, Ford, and the S&P 500 Index started to show very promising signs, and I couldn't help but contemplate what the future would hold if I could continue to make such genius selections (of course, not accurately recognizing how unique and non-replicable the 2008 situation was). However, my elation and self-satisfaction were soon reversed when something shook the markets that, despite spending hundreds of hours studying the topic, I didn't see coming at all: the European debt crisis.

By late 2009, the U.S. stock market had recovered from the lows and was starting to show signs of recovery. However, just when I thought that I could take some profits—and receive some praise and admiration for jumping into the stock market at one of the most favorable times to do so in the history of the U.S.—Europe's economy began to teeter on total collapse.

All across the continent, property values drastically deflated, unemployment shot up, and government bailouts were being demanded. In many respects, the situation in several European countries was significantly worse than it was in the U.S. For example, unemployment in Greece and Spain reached nearly 27%, and their government debt became truly unserviceable in its current form.[1]

These issues created severe market volatility. Economic uncertainty ripped through the global financial markets, causing many anxious investors in the U.S. to gear up for another 2008-esque situation. I was neurotically glued to the 24-hour news cycle, sometimes staying up until 2:00 a.m. to track updates from the European markets.

I remember watching CNBC in between classes when suddenly all of the anchors were focusing on one single metric: Greek bond yields. The biggest talking point was that if the yields for the Greek government's 10-year bonds remained below 7%, then the S&P 500 was going to remain at its current levels. However, if the yields went above that (now apparently) critical 7% benchmark, the S&P 500 was going to collapse.

---

1 www.cbsnews.com/news/eurozone-unemployment-at-record-high-in-may

The fear of impending doom in the global markets created colossal swings in the U.S. markets. Despite what most financial advisors may claim about how to achieve diversification, if panic sets in, stocks are going to fall across the board. During these times, if I actually slept through the night, it was not at all uncommon for me to wake up in the morning to find that my entire financial portfolio had fallen 5-7% overnight.

I couldn't believe that after all the hours I put in trying to educate myself on the stock market and economics, something as obscure, unpredictable, and uncontrollable as volatility in the Greek bond yields was playing such a significant role in my financial well-being.

As fate would have it, not only did these bonds surpass the aforementioned 7% hurdle, they would later go on to actually skyrocket up to nearly 30% at one point. Since bonds are essentially the rate at which a government can borrow money, Greece quickly became insolvent as it couldn't fund its liabilities or service its debt. Multiple bailouts and debt relief programs ensued along the way, which added more fuel to the dumpster fire taking place in all of the major stock markets in the world.

Watching CNBC while biting my nails as this catastrophe played out was my last-straw moment. From that point forward, I knew I needed to find an investment vehicle that was straightforward enough so the risks were significantly more understandable, predictable, and controllable. I needed to be able to get a solid eight hours of sleep and rest easy knowing that my portfolio wasn't being obliterated by unwieldy, seemingly irrelevant factors such as the interest rates of Greek bonds.

The pursuit to find that investment vehicle soon led me to real estate.

ENTRANCE INTO THE REAL ESTATE SECTOR

As an eager-to-learn investor but one who hadn't even opened his first real estate–specific book, I took the most common route into the real estate business back in those days: endless networking events.

For months, I spent three to five evenings each week at these meet-and-greets, navigating my way through Los Angeles, California during peak traffic hours trying to find a few key individuals with investment strategies I wanted to model.

An average evening looked like this: I'd spend a stressful hour driving to the event; pay the $20 entry fee; listen to a pitch about books, tapes, boot camps, and other educational products with varying degrees of useful information; get a few business cards from people I likely wouldn't follow up with; and call it a night.

While this strategy was certainly not the most efficient use of my time, I learned a lot from some key educational takeaways sprinkled throughout the pitches. More importantly, I was able to begin to build my network of like-minded real estate entre-preneurs, many of whom would eventually become my mentors. These few key players in the sector shared my worldviews, were focused on downside protection, and were looking to invest in vehicles that were well-positioned to perform in all stages of the economic cycle. With their guidance, I avoided some mas-sive pitfalls and learned to be patient enough to wait for those right-deal/right-time sweet spots. I almost certainly would have made some major mistakes in the beginning without their help.

My first real estate investments were made in 2011 in the form of hard money loans to a group of fix-and-flippers in the Memphis, Tennessee market. I would loan up to 80% of the purchase price to these seasoned flippers and create a mortgage that outlined the payment structure and specified that the single-family house being flipped would act as collateral for the loan. As the renovations took place, they would pay me monthly interest for the loan and, after the flippers renovated and sold the property, they would pay back my principal. If, for whatever reason, they defaulted on the monthly mortgage or were unable to repay the principal, I would take control over the home through the foreclosure process. In short, I was playing the role of the bank in the transaction.

At the time, I was able to receive 12% annual interest with 3% of the loan amount up front, resulting in a net annual return of 15-18%+ (depending on how long it took to fix and flip the property). To this day, those investments are still some of the most favorable risk-adjusted returns I've ever received because they were so well collateralized that I never worried about the borrower defaulting.

As more and more of these loans were successfully completed, I became enthralled by this system of investing, most notably because of the simplicity of the investment. Either the flipper paid me or they didn't, regardless of what was going on in the overall economy, and certainly unrelated to the Greek bond yields. Additionally, the investment was remarkably well-protected. Not only was the value of the collateral much higher than the size of the loan, the Memphis market was historically non-volatile, so the likelihood of the property value plummeting and putting my investment principal in a precarious situation was very low.

Genius, right? I assumed that either I'd stumbled into a license to print money, or the market was in a disequilibrium and these types of opportunities weren't going to last. Unfortunately, it ended up being the latter.

Throughout and directly after the Great Recession, access to liquidity in the fix-and-flip market dwindled. As the real estate and stock market started to stabilize around 2012, that liquidity started coming back. The interest rates of hard money loans, such as the one outlined above, went from 15%+ annualized down to approximately 8-9%. This lower return profile was far less compelling from my perspective, especially considering that the interest payments for these loans are taxed as income, bringing down the net return to the 5-6% range.

STEP INTO MY (SYNDICATED) OFFICE

As this change in the market unfolded and I continued to pursue superior returns while maintaining downside protection, I was introduced to the world of **syndicated investments**. These are investments in which investors pool their capital together to purchase higher-quality properties that would otherwise be unavailable to them. For example, if 100 investors each put up $50,000 into a syndicated investment, they could use that $5,000,000 cumulatively as a 33% down payment on a $15,000,000 property.

Usually, this structure is used for the purchase of commercial properties like multi-family apartments, self-storage facilities, shopping centers, and other large property types with high purchase prices.

In the syndicated investment structure, investors are typically passive partners who rely on an operating partner to execute the business plan. Operating partners are also referred to as operators, sponsors, and General Partners (GPs). I'll use these terms interchangeably throughout this book. The operator is the person or persons who's directly responsible for the execution of the investment. They interface with investors, brokers, and the property manager, and they're actively involved in the operational side of the investment, receiving a percentage of the investment's proceeds in exchange for completing these duties.

This structure appealed to me as an investor for many reasons, most notably because I could receive a large share of the opportunity's proceeds while relying on an expert to execute the business plan and handle the problems that would unquestionably arise. The more I learned, the more fascinated I became. When dealing with high-quality assets where the gross dollars are larger, the operators involved stand to gain millions of dollars. Therefore, they're more likely to be highly competent individuals who are more incentivized to focus on executing the business plan and less incentivized to try to skim a few hundred dollars here and there (something quite common in the management of single-family assets).

MOM-AND-POP OWNERS VS. TOP-TIER OPERATORS

The more moving parts there are in a particular investment vehicle, the more value a best-in-class operator can bring to the table. Therefore, if you're investing in a highly complicated asset class where a major market advantage can be created, the level of expertise a high-caliber operator can bring to a partnership can more than compensate for the portion of the proceeds they'll receive from the opportunity.

On the other hand, investing money in single-family houses is so common because it's relatively straightforward. If the property is rented, you're making money; if it isn't, you're not. That's pretty much it. Because of the simplicity of the investment vehicle, it's very difficult to achieve a true market advantage from your competitors. There just aren't enough ways to add value.

Compare this to a commercial asset class like self-storage. There are so many variables, such as pay-per-click advertisements, merchandise sales, relationships with truck-rental companies, marketing strategies, administrative fees, dynamic pricing models, data-driven buying models, and more. Each of these facets of the business further complicates the investment vehicle, creating the opportunity for a wide disparity between a mom-and-pop owner, who isn't sophisticated enough to implement all of these strategies, and a best-in-class operator, who has created an efficient system that optimizes each of these components of the business.

The business of commercial real estate is also highly scalable and rewards multi-property owners for a variety of reasons, making it even more advantageous to invest through a top-tier operator. Most notably, an operator can utilize significant economies of scale, allowing them to cut costs on insurance plans, property management fees, debt financing, and more.

By optimizing the systems and processes mentioned above and then applying those strategies across multiple properties, commercial real estate operators can create an even larger margin between themselves and mom-and-pop owners.

As these systems and processes become more and more optimized and as the economies of scale further benefit large firms (as opposed to single-asset owners), top-tier operators can produce significantly asymmetric returns for their passive investors, even when accounting for the fact that they're receiving a portion of the profits of the deal.

Because of the amount of value that can be created by proficient operators, the syndicated investment space can provide investors with the opportunity to consistently generate more lucrative returns, regardless of the market's timing. This is just one of the reasons I decided to build my career based on the syndicated real estate investment model—but more on that later.

Because of what I've outlined above, by late 2011, I'd started to steer away from single-family hard money loans and already had made several passive investments in syndications. The investments were generating predictable returns and things were going quite well.

But in reality, I hadn't yet even scratched the surface of what's possible in the world of real estate. I was missing a critical element that had the potential to turn my passion for real estate into a highly lucrative career: other people's money.

CHAPTER 2

My First Capital Raise

The doorbell rings.

I was so excited: After months of preparing my presentation on a mobile home park investment opportunity, my first guest had just arrived at my first investor luncheon. For the past two years, I'd been implementing this investing strategy for my own portfolio, built up an impressive track record, and solidified a partnership with a top-tier operating partner who was one of the most well-known mobile home park operators in the United States.

The year was 2013 and, even though the real estate market had started to show signs of strength, prices were still significantly depressed compared to historical standards. Due to the preponderance of mom-and-pop owners in the mobile home park business, there was an abundance of opportunities to buy mismanaged parks, then raise rents, cut expenses, and sell for lucrative gains.

From a data-driven perspective, the investment thesis was compelling. My track record had already provided proof of concept, and now the goal was to scale. This luncheon was the first step towards that goal.

I'd spent so much time preparing for this moment that I could give the entire 30-minute PowerPoint presentation with my eyes closed. I'd even recorded it and listened to myself give the presentation over and over again.

To get people in the door, I sent out emails to friends and family describing my success in the business. I also explained the strategic relationship with the operating partner who had already been involved in tens of millions of dollars of transactions and was in the process of raising their sixth fund. I made it clear that the systems, processes, and key members were already in place. The operating partner was simply rinsing and repeating, but they needed additional investor capital to do so.

My initial investments in syndications were for my personal portfolio, as well as the portfolios of my immediate family members. The next step was to share this investment opportunity with the next rung on my social and familial ladders, people with a significantly larger degree of separation.

Invitations were sent to a targeted group of people I thought might be interested and also had financial means to invest. I encouraged them to bring a friend as well. For reference, the bulk of invitees were my friends' mothers and fathers, their aunts and uncles, and a few of their friends.

I had no idea what the initial reception would be, but as more and more potential investors started to trickle in, my confidence grew; just having people attend was a major milestone.

I ordered catering for the guests and some wine to help ease nerves (and to loosen them up when it came time to close). There were about 30 attendees, a totally packed house. They were all accredited investors, meaning that they either made at least $200,000 per year or had a net worth of at least $1,000,000 excluding their primary residence. I did the mental math and was confident that there was at least $30,000,000 in the room. I certainly had never been in a room with that much investment potential in my career.

Even though I'd practiced the presentation hundreds of times, I admittedly started off a bit shaky. I thanked everyone for coming, gave a high-level overview of the presentation's structure, and noted that I'd be available for a Q&A session afterwards. Once I overcame the initial nerves, I settled in and things really started to flow.

The truth is, the mobile home park business sells itself. Here are some reasons why:

1. There are more than 10,000 baby boomers hitting the age of retirement every single day. Many have very little savings and rely on social security as their main source of income.[2] The average social security check is approximately $1,400/

---

2 www.pewresearch.org/fact-tank/2010/12/29/baby-boomers-retire; www.nhpfoundation.org/documents/FINAL%20RETIREMENT%20 CONFIDENCE%20SURVEY%203.20.pdf

month, while the average two-bedroom apartment in the U.S. rents for about $1,200/month.[3]

2. Municipalities throughout the country have all but banned the development of mobile home parks. This creates a uniquely favorable combination of an ever-increasing demand (primarily from baby boomers) and a contracting supply.

3. One of the keys to any real estate investment is to rent to tenants who treat your property like they own it, thus encouraging pride of ownership. When you invest in quality (3- or 4-star) mobile home parks, most of the tenants own the home they live in, and the park owner simply owns the lot underneath the home. Functionally, this has two major impacts on the business:

   a. Tenants who stay in these higher-rated parks prefer to own rather than rent, which attracts a highly desirable tenant base. This is in stark contrast to some of the horror stories you might have seen on television, which are typically 1- or 2-star parks.

   b. Tenants who own tend to stay longer and are much less likely to leave in the event that you raise rent.

Because of the unique and investor-favorable aspects of the business, investing in mobile home parks has recently become exceedingly popular in alternative investment circles. At the time of the presentation, back in 2013, there was far less interest in the space, and the opportunity was completely new and revelatory to

---

3 www.fool.com/retirement/2017/08/30/how-big-is-the-average-persons-social-security-che.aspx; www.abodo.com/blog/2018-annual-rent-report

this group of uninitiated investors. As I explained the compelling components of the mobile home park asset class as listed above and outlined the overall investment thesis of the offering, the attendees' interest was piqued. They started asking buying questions for which I was extremely well-prepared:

- How long is the hold period?
- When would we get our money back?
- Are you investing in the deal?
- What's your track record?
- When would I receive my first distribution?

Keep in mind, I'd been dedicated full-time to real estate investing for two years at this point and had spent an ample amount of time focused on the mobile home park business in particular. I'd conducted onsite visits with the operating partner across multiple states and had already proven with my own money that this team could execute their purposed investment strategy. In fact, during this time, I'd spent hundreds of hours conducting due diligence as an investor, asking questions far above and beyond what a typical investor would ask.

Not only was I bringing experience to the table, I could certainly hold my own when it came to closing a sale. I'd repeatedly proven this in my life.

Beginning at the entrepreneurial age of seven, I sold a litter of our dog's puppies to sweet ladies by assuring them, "You don't have to buy a puppy. Just hold the one you like the most and see how it makes you feel." How's that for pulling on the emotions of your potential buyer?

The summer after my freshmen year of college, I worked for Cutco, a direct sales company that sells high-quality cutlery. I led our branch in sales for the three consecutive months I worked at the company. As long as I had a product I believed in, I could effectively, passionately communicate in order to close deals.

Having confidence in my ability to close, I'd come to an agreement with the mobile home park operating partner that the investing entity (the entity in which I was pooling investors) would receive favorable terms only if I was able to raise and invest a minimum of $500,000 in the offering. If the raise resulted in less than that, the deal would not be economically viable, and all of the preparation and legal fees I'd already incurred would have been a waste of my time and money.

The real estate business is vast, but the world of passive syndications is incredibly tight knit; it especially was back in 2013. Word gets around about who delivers on promises—and who does not. I saw firsthand groups and investors get blacklisted from opportunities because they frequently made big promises and failed to deliver.

With this in mind, I was extra conservative in estimating that our group would invest at least $500,000. While I wasn't quite spending money I hadn't made yet, I was mentally congratulating myself for this remarkable achievement and starting this phase of my career with a bang.

The presentation went off without a hitch. Everyone was engaged and interested, I clearly communicated all of the compelling points of the investment, and I didn't miss a beat with the PowerPoint slides.

At the end of it, I asked the attendees to turn over the paper I'd placed in front of them. If they were interested in reserving an investment amount, I prompted them to write that figure down. Then, I asked that they flip the paper for privacy and hand it in to me. My intention was to get an idea as to what the commitment level was without pressuring attendees to raise their hand and share with the entire group.

And that was a wrap. I thanked everyone for coming and eagerly grabbed the pile of papers to calculate the results. Out of the 30 investment reservation documents, the total amount was—and you may have guessed it—$0.

Goose egg.

Naught.

Nil.

Nothing.

Zilch.

Zip.

Zero.

Nada.

Not one dollar.

This experience sent me on an emotional rollercoaster, the likes of which I'd never been through. Words can't accurately describe what this was like but "devastated" certainly comes to mind. I'd put so much effort into this presentation. My closest friends and mentors were eagerly awaiting my text to confirm that I'd achieved and, most likely, surpassed the $500,000 requirement.

Up until this point, I'd successfully invested my own money and helped close friends and immediate family invest. I was confident in my investment thesis, and I'd made a commitment to myself to pursue this career path for a variety of reasons, most notably because I'd fallen in love with the sector. It was a perfect fit for my personality, strengths, and lifestyle design. I'd been so sure of my ability to raise capital from interested parties and was completely destroyed.

My devastation was rooted in the high expectations I had set for myself, but also in the embarrassment of having to share this massive letdown with the friends and family, not to mention the operator, who believed in me. How could I positively spin this total flop? There was no easy way around it: The money wasn't coming through the door and we had a major problem.

What had gone wrong? Just to reiterate:

The investment thesis was solid, the track record was established, and I knew how to sell.

After a few weeks of absolute disappointment and distress, including endless hours quietly contemplating whether I should just go get a job at a traditional real estate firm (or give up on the sector completely), I started to piece together what went wrong.

THE MISSING FACTOR

Unfortunately, I'd not yet learned the single most important factor in determining entrepreneurial success: the ability to attract, nurture, and close high-quality clients. This is not exactly the be-all and end-all, but it's pretty close. If you're able to excel at this key facet of any business, you're *almost* guaranteed great success.

My confidence in raising $500,000 or more was based on the notion that the investment would be completely revolutionary to the attendees at the luncheon. Virtually none of them had any real estate investments, let alone in mobile home parks. However, the exact reason that I thought they were going to be blown away was exactly why no one decided to move forward.

The attendees weren't interested in these types of investments. If they had been, they would already have been investing in them, and they certainly wouldn't be hearing about them for the first time.

I retrospectively put myself in their shoes. Most were over 50 years old. They were accredited investors who had seen their portfolios grow consistently for the past 20 or 30 years, earning a reasonable 8-10% return. In order for them to take action, they'd have to sell stocks and move funds out of their brokerage account into our investment vehicle they didn't know anything about. This would require a huge shift in thinking about one of the most important components of their life: money. This major adjustment was supposed to take place during a 30-minute presentation, one led by someone much younger and likely with less investment capital than them?

This is exactly how it would be if someone were to give me a well-thought-out presentation on purchasing a dairy cow. They could make a really strong case that their particular cow completely outperforms market standards by producing 12% more milk than the competition. Not only that, it's being sold at a 40% discount.

"A 40% discount?" you might ask.

Correct, a 40% discount.

Who wouldn't be interested in a profitable, top-notch dairy cow at a 40% discount to market?

Me, that's who. Regardless of how compelling the thesis, regardless of the farmer's track record, and regardless of the fact that milk is in ultra-high demand, I have no interest in owning a cow.

In order to be successful in this real estate space, I needed an infrastructure to attract potential investors who were already interested in these topics and actively looking for these types of investments. Rather than swimming around aimlessly and hunting for fish with a harpoon, I needed to position myself like a bear at the top of the stream, waiting for the salmon to swim to me. I had to completely reverse my sales process. Instead of me chasing down potential leads, they needed to chase me.

If I could create a system like this, I was confident that any potential investor who found me would be much more likely to move forward, compared to someone I'd pestered into agreeing to a 30-minute phone call or another dreadful luncheon. If I could develop this infrastructure, it would allow me to acquire investors far more eager to invest over and over again. In short, I could attract the high-quality clients needed to make my business lucrative and scalable.

WHERE WE ARE TODAY

A lot has changed since that first attempt at raising capital. After countless hours dedicated to building the infrastructure I mentioned above and creating systems and processes that allowed the business to grow, I went from failing to raise $500,000 to raising $1,000,000, to $5,000,000, to more than $10,000,000 for a single offering. Cumulatively, this capital has allowed my firm, Asym Capital, to purchase more than $90,000,000 of commercial real estate across the United States.

In addition to the millions of dollars we (Asym) have raised for real estate offerings we believe in, I've been featured on more than 50 podcasts and published articles in *Forbes*, *Globe Street*, and *Inside Self-Storage*. I've also had the opportunity to interview and learn from more than 100 incredibly successful entrepreneurs on my own podcast, *Cash Flow Connections Real Estate Podcast*, including high-profile guests like Grant Cardone, Doug Casey, Cameron Herlod, and Tom Woods, as well as a variety of other economists, authors, and leading entrepreneurs.

Check out the podcast here: www.cashflowconnections.com/podcast

I also founded RaiseMasters, the #1 mastermind group for elite capital raisers. The mastermind is focused on helping real estate entrepreneurs, operators, and fund managers ensure that they never let a deal slip through their fingers due to lack of funding.

The mastermind consists of two monthly meetings, presentations from guest speakers, 10 hours of detailed capital raising training modules, and unlimited direct access to me.

My teaching and communication styles are unique and not for everyone. That said, if you resonate with the way in which this book is written, I'm confident you'd get a huge amount of value out of joining our mastermind.

Check out the mastermind here: www.raisemasters.com

To provide a more in-person flavor to our online education, we host an annual conference, the Intelligent Investors Real Estate

Conference (IIREC), which has been attended by hundreds of investors. The event brings together exceptionally experienced real estate professionals, property managers, economists, and thought leaders who have taken a deep dive into all aspects of the investment space. Not only is IIREC a great place to learn, it has also created an environment where meaningful professional relationships can be developed. Plus, the event is a lot of fun: We make sure of it! The event is produced by my wife Chrissy Thompson, founder of Dynamo Events, an event production company that has produced major high-end events everywhere from Los Angeles to Singapore.

Check out the conference here: www.intelligentinvestorsrec.com

All of these facets of the business work in sync to help us accomplish our company-wide goals, one of which is raising significant capital for our deals.

In this book, I'm going to dig deep into the most effective strategies to establish credibility, attract investors, and raise millions of dollars for your real estate offerings. This is the system you can use to secure the lifestyle you want (and the freedom that goes along with it) with the mindset of knowing that you won't need to scramble for capital every time you need to close. Trust me, I've been there—and I'm not going back any time soon.

WHAT THIS COULD MEAN FOR YOU

To be blunt: Raising capital is the most consistently sought-after skill in the entire real estate sector. Regardless of the specific aspect of the business you focus on, the ability to provide equity for your firm's purchases will always be needed and lucrative. Even if you're 100% dedicated to the operational and management side of real estate, being able to effectively communicate the value of a particular investment and raise seven figures will always be a desirable skill to have in your back pocket.

Do I have your attention? Great! But before I jump into the details of how to go about creating this infrastructure and raising private capital, I want to describe a moment when I realized how life-changing this skillset could be.

There's a well-known real estate crowdfunding firm that is, unquestionably, an industry leader in the sector. The firm is a venture capitalist (VC)–backed platform with close to 100 employees. It's a titan in the industry, one that spends millions of dollars each year on marketing, due diligence, software, and a variety of other enterprise-level services to maintain its position at the top of a very large mountain.

I follow this firm on social media and noticed a celebratory post that caught my attention. It was celebrating having raised a total of $200,000,000 across its offerings, an incredible accomplishment. When I saw this post, I began to fantasize about what it would be like to make such a serious impact on the real estate sector. I considered how many investors I could help if we were able to raise that sort of capital. I contemplated the neighborhoods that could be positively impacted by our operating partners going in and turning around dilapidated buildings. Keep in mind, if this firm raised $200,000,000 in equity, it likely used this money as a down payment with an additional $400,000,000 provided via debt financing—meaning they likely purchased $600,000,000 worth of commercial real estate. That valuation of real estate likely represented millions and millions of square feet of commercial property spanning across multiple cities, states, and regions.

Then, something even more powerful happened. A few short weeks after seeing that post, I was conducting due diligence on a new out-of-state offering. I'd flown across the country to meet the operating partner who had scheduled an entire day of onsite visits to different properties for me and several other potential capital partners. Over the course of the day with more than five hours of drive time, I really got to know the operator and the other capital raisers on an intimate level.

The SUV was filled with the who's who of private real estate syndication. I felt very lucky to be riding in the car, to say the least. The conversation about raising capital inevitably came up, and two individuals in the car (let's refer to them as Matt and John) revealed that they had each *personally* raised more than $100,000,000 of equity in the previous 10 years. They had cumulatively raised as much as that goliath VC-funded platform, yet they had a lifestyle that was completely in their control because they had no overhead or employees.

When I say that these two people had "individually" raised that amount of capital, I mean it in the truest sense of the word. I now know both Matt and John well, and neither of them has had more than an assistant on their team for the capital raising portion of their business. Now granted, the operational side of their businesses is completely different in terms of overhead, but when it comes to functionally raising capital, they each have effectively done this on their own while incurring only minimal costs.

I was certainly impressed with what the VC-funded crowd-funding platform was able to accomplish, but I never really wanted to be the CEO of a 100-employee company nor did I wish for the lifestyle that went along with it. Personal freedom has always been extremely high on the priority list, so running a very large firm has never been my true goal, nor has it been to need approval of a board of directors filled with VCs.

I've always found the idea of developing and maintaining an incredibly lean-and-mean team—one without bureaucracy, unnecessary meetings, or an HR department—far more compelling and correlated with an even better financial outcome. Not only would it be more advantageous to avoid a VC firm participating in the proceeds of my business, but I could also have the lifestyle design I truly desired.

Both Matt and John have dedicated thousands and thousands of hours to becoming absolute experts in their field, building up a personal brand, nurturing their leads, closing deals, and ensuring their investments perform.

Here's the thing though, from a personality perspective, Matt and John couldn't be more different. Other than the fact that they're both ultra-high performers in the real estate sector, they have very little else in common. In fact, many of their strengths and weaknesses don't even align. This was an important realization because it made me understand that as long as you have a few key ingredients, success in the industry isn't a one-size-fits-all recipe.

Not every high performer in real estate went to an Ivy League school. Not every real estate mogul is an excellent communicator. And so on and so forth.

It was at that point I realized that even though these two particular people clearly surpassed their peers in terms of results, they didn't necessarily have anything that I didn't when it came to the key ingredients for achieving greatness (which I'll talk about later in this book). I also realized that being in that SUV was a definite sign I was rubbing elbows with the right people.

These realizations, coupled with the momentum I'd gained by this time in my career, gave me confidence that I could reach that $100,000,000-raised milestone if I continued down this path. I'm confident you can too.

But nothing worth having comes easily. It hasn't been an easy ride for me so far, and it won't be for you either. There are myriad reasons why this industry is challenging and even more ways it can go wrong. First of all, the business is very lucrative and incredibly competitive as a result. Real estate constantly attracts the best of the best. Second of all, the challenges associated with the regulations surrounding investments are constantly burdensome. And lastly, it's one of the few industries where you can work your tail off for a few decades and, if you make a significant misstep, you can lose everything.

However, I'll address ways to mitigate these challenges and encourage you to consider the value of seeing this book through. Let's take the example of Matt and John. From a profitability standpoint, I would conservatively estimate that they're set to receive an average of 1.0% of their capital raised per year, assuming the investments they raised capital for perform as projected.

This would imply a $1,000,000 annual income for each individual from the performance of those investments alone, not including one-time acquisition fees, ongoing management fees, refinancing fees, disposition fees, et cetera, which could easily add up to an additional $2,000,000-$5,000,000, depending on a variety of factors. This amount of money all but eliminates any potential financial challenges they may face, and it has the potential to pay for a fairly remarkable lifestyle.

Yes, the real estate business has its challenges, but they're overshadowed by the many perks. Ever cruised around on a 131-foot yacht, taken a private jet to Las Vegas, or danced on a pool table in a 4,000-square-foot hotel penthouse? Because of the people with whom I've had the pleasure of working and the lucrative nature of the business, I can truthfully say I've done all of the above. Indulgences like this are fun and motivating, but for those who are philanthropically inclined, consider the ability that having a high-level income gives you to make a positive impact. Both Matt and John have chosen to leverage their financial position and network for the greater good by making considerable and inspirational contributions to charitable donations and taking time off for community-centric volunteer work. Perhaps just as importantly, they've graciously gifted others the playbook for how to achieve similar financial success and continue giving back.

For the last several years, I've studied the success of ultra-high performers in the industry, as well as ironed out systems and processes that work for me and the real estate company I've created. We have confirmed several times that our playbook works, and I want to share it with you. This book is my best, earnest attempt to help you create the pathway that'll provide you, your friends, and your family with the aforementioned financial and personal opportunities.

If this is of great interest to you, dog-ear Chapter 15: Paving the Road to $450,000 in Annual Income. You'll learn the mathematics of what it takes for you to achieve a high income level in this business. With incredible perseverance and focus, and a solid combination of **Key Momentum Indicators** (which you'll learn about in Chapter 3), achieving this type of success is absolutely possible. Trust me, the numbers aren't nearly as overwhelming as you may think.

Interested?

Good. Let's make it official.

ARE YOU READY TO COMMIT?

Some of you may read books just to pass the time. Some may read 52 per year like the average CEO (allegedly) does. Either way, you won't see results just from reading—you have to take action. I would be lying if I said that I don't frequently read just for entertainment, but the books that have had the biggest impact on my life were ones that outlined a blueprint for success and could be applied to my immediate action plan. My goal for you is that this will be one of those books, one that'll act as a map for your pursuit of raising money for real estate. In order to do so, you'll need to make the decision to read this book with that intention.

Now, don't misunderstand me. I don't want to disparage *anyone* who's taking the time to read this book. If you're here to pass the time on a trip, or you're listening to this on audio while you're in traffic and nothing is on the radio, or if you just think I'm a funny guy and are looking for comedic relief via intermittent jokes, that's no problem. Read at your leisure and a pace you think is best.

However, if you're reading this book because you actually want to implement the strategies, do us both a favor: Start blocking out time in your calendar so that you can finish this book in two weeks or less.

I've learned that most people, myself included, struggle to accomplish anything meaningful if they're not 100% focused on one thing for at least 60-180 minutes—especially if oscillating between different tasks. I've been able to overcome this by creating significant time blocks where duties can be batched, thus mitigating the cognitive fatigue associated with mentally shifting gears.

The book is about 60,000 words, which will take dedicated readers between six and eight hours of reading time to work through. Depending on how fast of a reader you are, go to your calendar and start scheduling those 60–180-minute time blocks until you're confident you have enough blocks to finish as quickly as possible.

Remember, distraction is the enemy of productivity. During these time blocks, you need to turn off your phone notifications, distance yourself from your computer, and steer clear of social media.

In this book, you'll learn, for instance, about the concept of **$2,000 Ideas**, which will be discussed soon. Before I get into the details, just know that the most meaningful takeaways you can get from educational content, from seminars to books (this one included), aren't derived from the actual content. The greatest takeaways are the ideas you extrapolate from the content on your own. You must read between the lines. Later in the book, I'll discuss ways to inspire these potentially lucrative inferences, but for now I'll present you with a time-honored trick. Take short (10-minute), uninterrupted breaks to contemplate the content you're reading. These breaks should take place every 60-120 minutes depending on your preference. Make sure to include those breaks in your calendar, ideally during and/or right after you read, in order to ensure you're prepared to dive in according to plan.

If you're ready to commit, schedule as many of these time blocks as needed with at least one or two 10-minute breaks built in. Then, be prepared to mentally download this book the same way Neo learned kung fu in *The Matrix*.

Are you ready to commit? Once you've made the decision to implement the strategies outlined in this book and blocked out uninterrupted time on your calendar, send me an email at hunter@raisingcapitalforrealestate.com and tell me that you're committed to learning, implementing, and eventually getting wealthy from these strategies. Also, make sure to include *why* succeeding in this sector is so important to you. I might even shoot you a free eBook or some other resources, just to show you how much I appreciate you taking this as seriously as I do.

CHAPTER 3

Financial Education:
The Ultimate Asymmetric Investment

T he name of our investment firm, Asym Capital, represents an abbreviated nod to **asymmetric returns**, a common expression in the investment space that's defined as favorably imbalanced or skewed returns in terms of **risk-return ratio.** Typically, when someone refers to an asymmetric return, it's because the return profile far exceeds the incurred risk, making it compelling for an investor on a risk-adjusted basis.

There's no better example of an asymmetric investment than an investment in financial education.

Prior to raising a nickel, you have to be highly knowledgeable in your sector and need to know who to trust in order to help protect and grow your investors' capital. Otherwise, you risk raising money for the wrong deal, with the wrong people, and under the wrong strategy. If your compensation is dependent on the performance of the investment (which it should be), you could end up costing your investors their hard-earned principal and unknowingly be working for free.

In this chapter, I'll review some of the key strategies and resources for accomplishing the first important step of raising capital for real estate: becoming an expert. We'll also talk about why both education and the resulting expertise are so specifically essential in the financial sector. Here are the main resources for getting started:

1. Financial education resources
    a. Podcasts
    b. Books
2. Networking Events
3. Mentorships
4. Mastermind Groups

FINANCIAL MISINFORMATION

When it comes to the world of finance, we in the United States are typically influenced by the media, educational systems, and cultural norms to view money as something both too private to discuss and too complex to understand. If we feel compelled to explore personal finance at all, we're told to consult a professional financial advisor who, in their omniscience, can be trusted to understand the intricacies of the global capital markets.

Due to the educational system's lack of focus on the matter, many people have misconceptions, limitations, and even anxiety about how to approach their investment portfolio, often resulting in unwise decisions. For example, hundreds of thousands of financial advisors take 0.5%-1.5% in annual **assets under management** fees for simply putting their clients' capital in a series of investments that are meant to track the market. (Of course, the investments are unable to achieve this stated goal due to the 0.5-1.5% annual loss from the financial advisor fees.) There are millions of people in the U.S. who pay these fees without realizing that they could simply hold an index fund and track the market with no financial advisor in the picture.

Case in point: A relative of mine recently contacted me regarding potential investment opportunities. I reviewed his financial portfolio which was being managed by a well-respected wealth manager. To my surprise, this financial advisor had selected one index fund which was purchased in 2001 and had not made a trade since, receiving a $20,000 annual fee for "managing the portfolio," although he was engaged in no active management at all. This is an egregious example, but it isn't totally unheard of in the world of finance. My relative, like most clients of investment advisors, was more focused on earning income at his job than monitoring his financial portfolio. Furthermore, he assumed, like most people would, that by hiring a professional money manager, surely he would fare better than if he were doing it himself, right?

Thankfully, technology is revolutionizing the financial industry in many ways. Online educational platforms are clueing people into the potentially extortionist nature of the financial advisor business and also allowing them access to incredible opportunities in the real estate market.

FINANCIAL EDUCATION RESOURCES

Podcasts: An Intimate Medium for the Productivity Seekers

The podcast medium has played a massive role in the education-based revolution within the financial sector. While other alternative media outlets have also significantly changed the general population's perspective on a lot of investment-related matters, the ability to learn while you drive, work, or work out has catapulted the podcast sector to the next level, especially when it comes to alternative investments like real estate.

I'm proud to say that we've contributed to the thinking of tens of thousands of investors through our show, the *Cash Flow Connections Real Estate Podcast*. Our program is an informative resource that features in-depth interviews with high-profile authors, economists, investors, and capital raisers as guests, all of whom have added tremendous value to our listener base.

The show's mission is to help investors protect and grow their capital. Sometimes, fulfilling this mission means taking a skeptical approach to investing and even sometimes suggesting that investors pass on certain opportunities. This is definitely antithetic to why most people host an investing podcast, but it's something that I feel is lacking in the financial education space.

Of course, our show is only one of many real estate–related podcasts. My suggestion is to find a few favorite shows that you really identify with and make sure to never miss an episode. With so much noise out there, there's true value in going deep rather than wide. Also, this way, you won't be simultaneously bombarded with different investment perspectives and feel like you don't know which direction to go.

Below are a few programs that consistently put out quality content:

- *Best Real Estate Investing Advice Ever*
- *Apartment Building Investing*
- *The Real Estate Guys™ Radio Show*
- *Investing in the U.S.*
- *Lifetime Cash Flow Through Real Estate Investing*
- *How to Lose Money*
- *The Investor Mindset Podcast*
- *The Real Estate Syndication Show*

These are well-established podcasts, but the space is evolving every day. Since this book was written, I'm sure excellent players have since entered the arena. Do some research. Identify the best people in your particular niche and go all-in on their free content.

Before spending time and money on coaching and mentorship—and especially before you invest in anything—I highly suggest that you spend 25-50 hours listening to podcasts and increase your level of education about what's available out there. With so much educational information at your fingertips, there's no reason to rush this process.

Books

In addition to podcasts, several books have significantly shaped my worldview and perspective as an investor. These are the ones I found most influential and deserving of attention in the real estate and entrepreneurship spaces.

Real Estate, Investing, Sales, and Negotiation:

- *Rich Dad Poor Dad: What the Rich Teach Their Kids About Money That the Poor and Middle Class Do Not!,* by Robert T. Kiyosaki
- *Mastering the Market Cycle: Getting the Odds on Your Side,* by Howard Marks
- *The Due Diligence Handbook For Commercial Real Estate: A Proven System To Save Time, Money, Headaches And Create Value When Buying Commercial Real Estate,* by Brian Hennessey
- *Principles: Life and Work,* by Ray Dalio
- *Pitch Anything: An Innovative Method for Presenting, Persuading, and Winning the Deal,* by Oren Klaff
- *Never Split the Difference: Negotiating as if Your Life Depended on It,* by Chris Voss

Non-Real Estate:

- *Double Double: How to Double Your Revenue and Profit in 3 Years or Less,* by Cameron Herold
- *Clockwork: Design Your Business to Run Itself,* by Mike Michalowicz

- *How an Economy Grows and Why It Crashes,* by Peter Schiff
- *Economics in One Lesson: The Smartest and Surest Way to Understand Basic Economics,* by Henry Hazlitt
- *What Has Government Done to Our Money,* by Murray M. Rothbard
- *Own the Day, Own Your Life: Optimized Practices for Waking, Working, Learning, Eating, Training, Playing, Sleeping, and Sex,* by Aubrey Marcus
- *The Charisma Myth: How Anyone Can Master the Art and Science of Personal Magnetism,* by Olivia Fox Cabane
- *Deep Work: Rules for Focused Success in A Distracted World,* by Cal Newport

Each of these books is filled with useful content, so pick a few on topics you find most interesting and dive in. As I mentioned earlier in this chapter, the risk-return ratio for financial education is extremely favorable, so the time you invest in this reading list will not be wasted.

NETWORKING EVENTS

It's possible to acquire a post graduate–level understanding of real estate by dedicating yourself to education through podcasts, books, and paid courses. But the truth is, that knowledge won't get you far without strong, trust-based relationships. As the old adage goes, **"Your network is your net worth."**

At the end of the day, you're probably considering investing in and raising capital for illiquid investments with five- to ten-year hold periods. Because of this, you and your investors will rely on other individuals to deliver way down the road. Plus, your operating partner's ability to exit the property with a favorable valuation at some point will be a major determining factor in your compensation, given that most real estate compensation is heavily weighed on the backend to align your incentives for long-term performance.

My point? In order to be successful in real estate, you need both knowledge and a reliable team. The best way to begin building your network is by attending live, in-person events with a specific focus on networking. Because attending events can be time consuming and yield little results, you need to have a clear plan of attack.

$2,000 Night or Bust

I have a love/hate relationship with in-person networking events. I essentially started my career by attending upwards of five networking events each week, and I almost certainly wouldn't be nearly as successful without going through that phase. However, there was undoubtedly a point where I really wasn't seeing a positive ROI on time spent going to event after event. Keep in mind, the $20-$50 ticket price was trivial when compared to the hours spent researching new events, navigating traffic in Los Angeles (not to mention parking), and getting endlessly pitched on other "higher-level" educational boot camps.

Later in my career, when my time became much more valuable, I came to this simple realization:

If an in-person event doesn't have the potential to bring $2,000 worth of value to my business, allowing me to have what I call a **$2,000 Night**, my time would be better spent focusing my efforts on something that could.

How can you define $2,000 in value? Before any event, you have to be crystal clear about the concepts, relationships, and resources that'll help take your business to the next level.

Dan Sullivan, founder and president of Strategic Coach says, "Our eyes can see and our ears can hear only what our brain is looking for."

This means that if you take the time to classify what needs to happen for you to receive $2,000 worth of value, you'll be much more receptive when the opportunity presents itself.

Before any event, take 10 minutes to brainstorm what you would need to take away in order to consider the evening a $2,000 Night. From my perspective, there are two main ways to have a $2,000 Night: get a **$2,000 Idea** or make a **$2,000 Contact**.

Let's start with $2,000 Ideas.

Here are a few examples of key takeaways that can instantly make your night out well worth it:

- Due diligence processes that experts are implementing
- Actionable marketing tactics
- Books to read
- Regulations to be aware of
- Market conditions that impact your business
- Information about another networking event that's in close alignment with your investment focus
- Any idea that could directly make or save you $2,000 or more

How applicable each of these are to your current business will vary, but taking the time to iron out your main focus will make your eyes widen and your ears perk up when these topics arise. Because the real estate business is very lucrative, one key takeaway from a networking event can easily result in a successful $2,000 Night. As long as, of course, you implement it. Remember, the challenging thing about $2,000 Ideas is that they often aren't explicitly identified as such. To a certain extent, you have to recognize them and bring them into reality.

A perfect example: I was at a networking event and met an operator who ran an ATM company. My ears perked up because I know ATMs are historically quite recession-resistant, which is an important component of my investment thesis. I was interested in investing, so I basically redirected the entire conversation to focus on ATMs. As we were talking, however, I discovered a few challenges. First, the ATM market is very saturated, which means it's frequently hard to find locations in which to place them. Then I learned that the operator wasn't taking on additional capital from investors because they were so backlogged with investment commitments.

I was a bit disappointed, but before the conversation ended, the operator gave me some good advice. He suggested that if I was interested in alternative investments like ATMs, I should attend this other networking event in West Los Angeles that specifically focused on niche cash flow–focused investments.

Ding-ding-ding! A $2,000 Idea!

I researched the event, bought my ticket, and showed up. It was here that I met Jeremy Roll, the host of the meetup, who ended up being one of the most influential people in my real estate career. Jeremy has not only been a mentor of mine since day one but has partnered with me on many opportunities over the years. In fact, we've been involved in tens of millions of dollars' worth of transactions together. There's a reason why the very first interview on the *Cash Flow Connections Real Estate Podcast* is with none other than Jeremy Roll himself.

When the ATM operating partner explained that his firm wasn't taking on additional investor capital, I could've just checked out of the conversation and moved on with my life, but I was striving for that $2,000 Idea, so I took his suggestion seriously. As a result, I established a critical relationship.

Identifying $2,000 Ideas

The most significant $2,000 Ideas aren't recognized when they're simply planted in front of you. They're understood through preliminary preparation and upon deeper contemplation. (This is why so many epiphanies come in the shower.)

The ATM operator didn't say, **"Hunter, pay attention. It's very important that you attend the networking event I'm referring to because it'll likely catapult your career to the next level."** It was something that I inferred from the discussion because I knew what I was looking for.

Let's think back to Christopher Nolan's movie *Inception*. A major plotline in the film is the theory that in order to make an idea really stick in someone's head, they have to feel like they came up with it on their own. To a certain extent, I've come to agree. **Some of the best ideas you'll get from this book aren't written on the pages but come from what you infer from the content.**

As you might recall from Chapter 2, one way to inspire these self-incepted ideas is to take short, 10-minute breaks, digesting the information and contemplating what you've learned. Research shows that non-cognitively demanding tasks, such as walking, knitting, or doing the dishes, can stimulate profound ideas because these kinds of tasks keep you engaged as you process the material without maxing out your entire cognitive ability.

When you get home from a networking event, or even the next morning, carve out time to contemplate what you learned and ask yourself, "What takeaways did I stumble upon that could give me the next big idea I've been looking for?"

As I mentioned, for these 10-minute breaks to be successful, it's absolutely critical that you avoid interruptions so that you can enter into a state of deep thought.

Creating Your Rolodex of $2,000 Contacts

Valuable concepts are amazing, but real estate is a team sport. Great investment ideas will be useless if you don't have a network to help implement them. This is where $2,000 Contacts come in.

As you brainstorm what your $2,000 Night should look like, you should also think about what types of contacts could really take your career to the next level and make a list of the archetypes that come to mind. Completing this exercise will tune you into the $2,000 Contact wave frequency.

Here is a non-specific list of contacts that could be worth $2,000 down the road:

- Investors
- People who could refer investors to you
- Real estate operators
- Brokers
- Excel modeling experts
- Wholesalers
- Potential business partners
- Experts in an asset class you're interested in
- Leaders of networking groups
- Authors of real estate books

Some of these may apply to you, some may not. Either way, make a point to avoid a vague, wide-ranging list. It should include the types of contacts that you actually need to propel your business to the next level.

One key difference between successful real estate entrepreneurs and everyone else is their ability to leverage relationships to grow their business and solve problems if something goes wrong. Effective networking skills and the ability to acquire quality team members are critical. I promise this: If you take this part of your business seriously, the results will speak for themselves.

Bonus: Becoming the $2,000 Connector

Early on in a conversation at a networking event, it'll often be clear that a particular person is **not** going to meet any of the requirements you previously outlined. If this happens, don't check out. Rather than trying to politely end the conversation, **listen to what they're looking for.** Think about the types of $2,000 Contacts they might need in order to have a $2,000 Night.

Connecting someone else with a $2,000 Contact should be half of your goal at any given networking event. Why? First of all, it feels great to help other people achieve their real estate goals. Second of all, reciprocity is a natural human impulse, and it's highly likely that anyone you introduce to a $2,000 Contact will be compelled to do the same for you. Once you start implementing this strategy consistently, others will introduce you to your $2,000 Contacts automatically. This helps you get the best result out of attending live events and scale your business quickly.

Because I'm am fully focused on commercial real estate, I no longer deal with single-family residential (SFR) investments very frequently, so it's easy to mentally check out of a discussion with an SFR operator if it's clear that there's no real overlap in our businesses. However, if I find myself talking with someone who's interested in investing hard money loans for single-family properties, I make a mental (or physical) note to introduce them to any fix-and-flipper I meet that night. If I do meet said flipper, I ensure that the two meet each other. If the connection is made, it could be a $2,000 Night for both of them.

Granted, it takes practice to become a stellar networker and connector. At first, you might be too shy to introduce two strangers you just met, especially in person. Try to take your ego out of it—after a few successful introductions, it'll feel natural and you'll realize just how rewarding it is.

I want to clarify this: The goal is not to introduce 25 people to another 25 people who may or may not be a good fit. If you do that, you start to become the type of person that is just "spraying and praying" contacts. This is much better than the business card spray-and-pray strategy because it's clearly not as self-serving, but if your introductions aren't thoughtful, they don't pack any punch.

Once you've deemed it appropriate to facilitate the introduction, make 100% certain that they meet each other, never assuming they'll take the initiative to follow up on their own. Some networking attendees might not even take action if you exclaim, "You have to meet this SFR operator; he is right over there!" So, physically walk them over and make the introduction to ensure that the two parties get connected.

Additional Tips for Networking

Unlike the stock market world, you cannot simply sit behind a computer, click a mouse, and make millions in this industry. You have to build your network to grow as a real estate investor and capital raiser. Here are some additional tips for navigating networking events and getting the most bang for your buck:

1. **Only attend events you can see yourself attending for at least six consecutive meetings.** Regardless of your attitude and networking skills, you'll get zero results if you attend sporadically. Even if you're the most naturally charismatic person in the world, people will only feel comfortable enough to do business if they're familiar with you.

2. **Show up early.** By doing so, you can capitalize on one of the most important parts of the night: the networking opportunity prior to the presentation or content portion of the event. Additionally, showing up early will help you complete networking tip #3.

3. **Get to know the host(s).** This is usually the person(s) with the most knowledge and social status, in terms of the event's dynamics. If you're able to strike up a conversation with them, you'll likely walk away with a $2,000 Idea. Also, if you're there early, you're far more likely to be perceived as the type of person that others will want to introduce themselves to, significantly increasing your chances of meeting a $2,000 Contact.

4. **Start a conversation with the first person you see.** For many, in-person networking can be a bit intimidating, as meeting and engaging with new people can be a challenge. One way I've found to overcome this is to implement a five-second rule: As soon as you walk in the door, introduce yourself to someone within the first five seconds. This will give you some momentum to carry through the remainder of the event.

5. **If you attend a meeting that's not a good fit, move on.** Many events out there are simply pitch fests with no real meaningful content. These types of events will mostly be attended by inexperienced investors who are just trying to find a route to enter the business. If something feels off, just keep searching for a core group of people that you feel comfortable with. Once you tap into this core group, it's like a domino effect: Their networks will include the

types of people you'll want to connect with as well, exponentially expanding your network.

My favorite site for finding local networking events is Meetup (www.meetup.com), and I personally built my network almost exclusively from the For Investors By Investors (FIBI) community, which posts its events at www.forinvestorsbyinvestors.com.

I tend to prioritize productivity, so the time and energy spent getting through traffic for less-than-par content felt burdensome. However, I came to realize the importance of the relationships I created at these sorts of events and now cherish the contacts I've made over the years. In fact, a few key individuals I met early on have propelled my career to heights that would have been unreachable had I simply stayed on the couch reading infinite real estate books and listening to thousands of hours of podcast interviews.

Don't make the mistake of thinking it's all about educational content. To be successful in this business, you'll absolutely need a team you can depend on. If you take the suggestions above seriously and develop a clear game plan, you'll be able to streamline the time you spend networking so you can acquire that team as quickly as possible.

MENTORSHIP

Every high-performing real estate entrepreneur I know has at least one specific individual who played a significant role in their success. In order to catapult your career to an ultra-expert level, you'll unquestionably need a minimum of one person on whom you can rely to guide you through challenging situations, the kind of guidance you just can't find in a textbook.

When it comes to mentorship, I was very fortunate for a variety of reasons. First of all, I entered the real estate arena in 2010, immediately after one of the most significant real estate collapses in U.S. history. Based on historical standards, it was one of the most favorable times to begin a career investing in the sector.

However, it wasn't just the deflated values that made the timing fortuitous. I'd also just moved to California, one of the states hit hardest by the Great Recession. Because of the severity of the collapse in real estate in California, many of the people who were attending networking events at the time were the people who had weathered the storm economically. They were the very few who had created investment strategies that protected their capital through the crash. Essentially, the market collapse had filtered out a ton of the noise, and because of that, I was able to network with the best of the best very quickly.

As I mentioned previously, one key individual whom I met early in my career was Jeremy Roll, President of Roll Investment Group. Jeremy is a Wharton Business School graduate, full-time passive investor, and significantly influential person in the world of passive investing.

It became clear during our first conversation that we had a very similar perspective in terms of the investment sector, but he already had experience and success actually implementing the strategies I felt were most compelling. During that initial meeting, I saw that I needed his guidance to supercharge my learning curve by leveraging his knowledge and expertise so I wouldn't have to figure it all out on my own.

Over the next few months, I would frequently reach out to Jeremy to share investment opportunities I was receiving to get a sense of his perspective on the offerings. We eventually began scheduling recurring calls during which we would review deal after deal, analyze different asset classes, and discuss the state of the economy. Brick by brick, these calls built upon the foundation of my perspective as an investor. To this day, I'm still very grateful for them.

So, how can you facilitate a similar relationship for your own business? Just like the pre-networking event brainstorming session discussed previously, the first step is to clearly outline exactly what you're looking for so that you can be tuned in when the opportunity presents itself.

Someone with whom you could conduct future business might be a $2,000 Contact, but a mentor holds priceless value. A mentor will thoughtfully guide you through critical decisions, help you navigate challenging situations, and likely play a huge role in your career. Because of the nature of this relationship, it's critical to identify someone you admire and intuitively trust, someone with whom you see eye-to-eye, and someone you could imagine as a close friend over 10 years from now. Here are a few things to look for in a potential mentor:

1. They're an absolute expert in their field.
2. The way they already operate in the business is very close to your ideal position in the sector.

3. You two see eye-to-eye naturally. If it's not an amazing personality match, the relationship won't last and, therefore, will not yield results.
4. They're bringing a tremendous amount of value to the table. This is especially important if you're paying for the mentorship. This includes:
   a. Processes and systems
   b. Team members for outsourcing work
   c. Deal analysis
   d. Deal flow
   e. Networking opportunities

Cumulatively, these qualities make up an excellent mentor. Now that you've seen them articulated, you'll be much more tuned in to find the person to fill that role.

Inspiring Mentors Through Key Momentum Indicators

There will be asymmetry in the beginning of any real estate mentor/mentee relationship. Inherently, you won't bring as much to the table as they do, but that's the whole point. Even if you pay them for their mentorship, an imbalance will still exist because most successful real estate entrepreneurs don't make the bulk of their money mentoring. The real question is this: How do you overcome that reality and inspire ultra-high performers to invest their time in you and share the trade secrets that got them to where they are today?

You have to show them that you possess something every high performer is absolutely addicted to: momentum.

To attract and inspire a high-quality mentor, you have to explicitly and intentionally display what I call the **Key Momentum Indicators** (KMIs). The KMIs are easily recognizable traits that show those around you that you're unstoppable, that either people need to get on board or get out of your way. Every high achiever can relate to this mindset because it's exactly what got them to where they are today. When high performers see that you're displaying these rare traits, they'll immediately recognize a reflection of themselves and be attracted to your potential, creating a connection that'll inspire them to help you achieve your goals through their mentorship. Here are the KMIs, the most important traits that'll attract the mentor of your dreams:

1. **Sense of urgency to accomplish your goals.** In E66 of the *Cash Flow Connections Real Estate Podcast*, "Creating and Nurturing Relationships with People of Influence," Jamie Smith shares the single most important character trait that inspires high performers to build a relationship with you: the ability to display an undying, unwavering sense of urgency to accomplish your goals. This sense of urgency, combined with a rock-solid plan of execution, is the most important determining factor of success. By intentionally demonstrating this trait, you'll create the notion that you're going to succeed, it's just a matter of who wants to come along for the ride. This is incredibly attractive to high performers, because so few people have this attitude.

2. **High speed of execution and implementation.** The faster you can take an idea from a concept to a fully executed project, the higher the probability is that you're going to

be successful. I've mentored dozens of students, and the ones who take projects from ideas to completion quickly are the most likely to succeed. For example, let's say I have a conversation with a student in my mentorship program, and we both agree that they need to set up a limited liability company (LLC). If I receive an email four days later that the LLC is ready for business, I'm 99% certain they'll be successful going forward. Other successful people pick up on that as well. Want to know why? Success compounds similarly to the way investments compound over time. The rate at which you'll compound success is based on your speed of execution. Also, speed takes courage, and courage alone can make up for many weaknesses in other areas.

3. **Attention to detail and high demand for excellence.** Many millions of dollars can be made—or lost—in real estate. Small mistakes can be catastrophic. Before sending an email, issuing a quarterly report, or making an offering available to investors, every detail should be triple checked. Excel formulas should be confirmed, properties should be toured, and typos should be non-existent. Practice this if it doesn't come naturally to you or hire help. Trust me, it's necessary. Working at this level requires the will-do-anything attitude it takes to provide the highest quality for any given project.

4. **Obsession with growth.** Few things attract momentum like someone who is obsessed with constantly taking their career to the next level. While it's important to recognize your accomplishments to avoid burnout, you should never be complacent with your personal and professional growth.

Make it clear that you're always striving for bigger and better things because that is what successful people do as well. Imply that you're always trying to level-up your network, finding the "best-in-class" to rub shoulders with. After all, this attitude is what led you to them, and there's nothing wrong with subconsciously stroking anyone's ego.

5. **Curiosity about new topics and a desire for expertise.** Due to the real estate sector's scalability, relatively small teams can accomplish remarkable things. However, this requires individual team members to wear multiple hats with a high degree of excellence. Because of this, you need to be able to learn new, challenging skills frequently and quickly to become an expert in them. Just having this trait isn't enough though. You also have to make it clear to those around you. To do this, when you're presented with an interesting, counterintuitive, or challenging idea, make it clear that you're curious about learning more. Ask questions, show interest, and most importantly, follow up once you've learned more on your own and can engage in the conversation at a higher level. This is a really powerful KMI and I almost never hear people talk about it.

Any trait without another is fairly meaningless. If you have an obsession with growth but put forth sub-par work, the value that you're bringing to any reputable mentor is extremely limited. If you have an eye for detail and produce high-quality work but fall into analysis paralysis and can't take action, you can't be relied on to execute or close a transaction. Especially if you're asked to complete a task for a potential mentor, you should blow them away, both with the speed of execution and the quality of work.

If you're able to authentically display high KMIs to potential mentors, you'll find that you're able to attract the best and brightest, and your career will quickly gain momentum. The help of these key individuals will push you along, snowballing your career, and help you navigate challenging situations as they arise. Furthermore, when you start to involve other high performers who are, to a certain extent, investing in you, the amount of accountability increases drastically. This makes your success less dependent on your sheer will and more of a team effort.

Successful people are always looking for ways to grow their businesses, and a younger, hungrier, more enthusiastic version of themselves makes a much better ally than a competitor. Also, at the end of the day, high performers have a very healthy relationship with competition. Many want to be considered the best of the best, not only in terms of the size of their bank accounts, but also the positive influence they have on the world. Helping new real estate entrepreneurs can be a great vehicle to accomplish both goals, as they can potentially create a future partner while positively impacting someone else's life. Don't be afraid to use this to your advantage.

MASTERMIND GROUPS

Another way to effectively learn from others is to join or start a mastermind group. This is a group of likeminded individuals who can leverage each other's experience to gain vast knowledge and rapidly achieve their similar desired results.

If you plan to attend a mastermind group, many of the suggestions for networking events will also apply; refer back to them for guidance.

If you plan on starting your own, here are a few tips for creating an impactful real estate mastermind group:

1. **Launch with a critical mass.** Attendees' first impressions are crucial. In order to ensure that you start off with a bang, leave plenty of lead time so that you can conduct extensive marketing efforts prior to your first meeting. Take time to go to networking events, create an online event page, and dedicate some time to ensuring a minimum of 10 people show up at the first event. Keep in mind that many people won't make all of the future events, so starting off with a larger pool of attendees is important.

2. **Remember that consistency is key.** Don't establish a mastermind group's schedule that you can't keep for at least six months. From my perspective, this is the shortest amount of time in which you can truly identify if it's worth your energy or not. Weekly meetings may not be sustainable because even though you may be passionate and have a flexible schedule, others will quickly drop off. Monthly or quarterly meetings have a far higher likelihood of long-term sustainability, which is what really counts.

3. **Ensure that the schedule is replicable and does not require too much work on your end.** One good example of this is a monthly business book review club. Yes, you'll have to read one book per month—but the books are already written. Another potential idea is to have a guest speaker every meeting. That way, the guests provide the content, as

opposed to you. This is far less of a time requirement than a mastermind structure in which you give a presentation every month, for example. Every meeting should follow a similar structure so you don't have to plan a brand-new agenda every time.

4. **Just starting out and still want to create a mastermind group? I strongly suggest focusing the content around other people's expertise rather than your own.** An industry-wide faux pas is when novices provide investment advice to a mastermind group before they're ever successful in real estate. To clarify, don't let inexperience alone deter you from starting one. Just be clear with your audience that the value of the mastermind is provided by other high performers in the industry, such as guest speakers or other peoples' books, and that you're there to learn as well. There's nothing wrong with that.

From a credibility standpoint, it can be very beneficial to run your own mastermind group, but if you're just getting started, I strongly suggest joining one that already exists. Another option is to volunteer at an existing mastermind group. This would provide you with some of the credibility, as well as foster a relationship with the mastermind founders.

RaiseMasters—The #1 Mastermind Group for Elite Capital Raisers

There are many real estate coaching programs and mastermind groups out there, but almost none of which specifically focus on raising capital. This is shocking to me, given that raising money is the single greatest determining factor of whether or not a real estate firm has the ability to scale successfully.

Additionally, many real estate entrepreneurs experience some initial success (typically relying on friends and family to fund their first deals), only to find that their original capital sources have dried up at the exact moment that they were ready to take their careers to the next level.

Why? Because they haven't focused their efforts on answering the most important question in the capital raising business:

How can I turn ice-cold leads into raving fans, who later turn into repeat $100,000+ investors?

Few recognize it, but that's the question real estate entrepreneurs should be asking if they're interested in going from $1 million under management to $100 million under management.

In order to provide all my answers to that very question, I created RaiseMasters, a mastermind for real estate entrepreneurs, capital raisers, and fund managers who are ready to scale their real estate business—but just need additional capital to do so. The program gives its members an over-the-shoulder look at everything we do at Asym Capital. We provide our members with the exact systems, processes, email templates, apps, closing scripts, and service providers that have allowed Asym to raise tens of millions of dollars.

We've perfected this truly plug-and-play template, and our members repurpose and reuse it for their respective real estate businesses. And it works. In fact, we've helped our members consistently raise millions of dollars, over and over again.

Plus, each month, a real estate heavy hitter comes to present to our group and gives away all their capital raising secrets as well.

Because of the results we've seen our members achieve and the electric energy that's created when you get a group of likeminded self-starters in a room together, RaiseMasters has become something I'm really proud of.

Here are the training modules that come with the mastermind membership:

(Please note that we're always making changes to the program to increase value; these modules are subject to change.)

1. Capital Raising Pre-Training
2. Setting Up Your Scalable Capital Raising Business
3. Who and Where Are Your Dream Investors?
4. Grow Your List, Scale Your Portfolio
5. Educating and Nurturing Your Investors to Streamline Your Capital Raising Process
6. Closing Investor Funds
7. Unlocking the Fund of Funds Model
8. Institutional Millions: The Secrets to Receiving $10 Million Checks from One Investor
9. Your Capital Raising Compliance Blueprint
10. Paving Your Road to $100 Million Raised

While the subject matter is related to this book, the 10+ hours of highly detailed modules exclusively contain all-new and never-before-seen content.

If you want to learn more, visit www.raisemasters.com.

CHAPTER 4

Creating Your Perfect Real Estate Investment Team

O ne of the reasons that so much focus is put on networking in the previous chapter is that you simply must build a team in order to achieve significant success in the real estate sector. Your team is the infrastructure by which you can create systems and processes that'll result in you and your company experiencing growth and profitability. However, it's absolutely critical that you not only select the right team members, but that their role in the company accelerates your progress, rather than impedes it. They need to take certain responsibilities off your plate so you can focus on the parts of the business you're truly gifted at. Balancing all of these components together is what makes a real estate company work smoothly.

IDENTIFYING A HIGH-QUALITY OPERATING PARTNER

Once you've gained confidence in your understanding of the real estate sector through the strategies outlined earlier in Chapter 3, it's time for you to pursue live investment opportunities. One of the most efficient ways to get this process started is to leverage the existing deal flow of an operating partner who already has a background in this business.

It's very common for small real estate firms to have two main principals/partners: one who focuses primarily on the investor-relations side of the business, conducting capital raising duties, talking to investors, et cetera, while the other partner focuses on the operating side of the business and the implementation of the business plan. There may be cross-over between the two, but this is generally the division of labor for most real estate firms.

You're reading this book, and you've made it this far, so I'll assume that you consider (or want to consider) raising money to be a significant portion of what you bring to the real estate table. If that's the case, I strongly suggest that you align yourself with an operating partner who can focus their efforts on the operational side of the business.

At Asym Capital, our system for identifying, conducting due diligence on, and curating high-quality operating partners is a huge value-add to our investor base. To date, I've likely spent 10,000 hours working on this system, the very system that has allowed us to work with some of the best operators in the real estate business. However, because this book is focused on raising capital, we're going to keep this section as high-level as possible.

Keep in mind, though, it's absolutely critical that you work with an all-star operating partner. If you don't, your offerings will not perform, and success will be unattainable. I'll trust that you really delve into this topic before partnering with anyone on a deal.

With that said, here are a few tips for identifying a high-quality operating partner:

1. **Read between the lines when conducting due diligence on the operating partner. Remember that all of your efforts should focus on discerning whether or not they're the type of person/personality you're comfortable making a bet on.** They may have the most sophisticated systems and incredibly impressive business acumen, but do they align with you ethically? Jeremy frequently says, "Even if you invest in a property in Beverly Hills, California that's 100% occupied, if the operating partner commits fraud, all of the investors will likely lose money." Don't forget that.

2. **Choose a partner with direct and considerable experience in this business but who can be flexible in terms of compensation for you as a capital raiser.** You should never bring capital to a deal with an operating partner who doesn't have a significant track record in the business. There should never be a learning curve with your investors' capital—or your own capital for that matter. This sometimes poses a challenge, because highly experienced operators with a proven track record may not have a need for additional investor capital. You certainly don't want to go into a business venture without leverage to negotiate. Be mindful

of the important balance between the significance of the operating partner's track record and their willingness to be flexible and create a structure that works for you.

3. **Get an understanding of whether or not their systems are already established or if significant business changes will need to be made in order to implement their business plan.** Thoroughly understanding the unknowns is critical as an investor, so get a solid sense of whether they're in the process of simply rinsing and repeating their previous successes or if this venture will require testing out new strategies. This makes a big difference in the risk profile of the partnership.

4. **Talk to their professional referrals.** Understandably, a large focus is put on an operating partner's previous investors. However, I've gained much greater insight into the potential partner's current business by talking to their accountants, attorneys, property managers, contractors, and insurers. This also helps with vetting for ethical and personality fits.

5. **Run a background check.** This is one of the most under-utilized and easiest ways to look into the operating partner you're considering working with. Prior to running the background check, ask the operating partner if there's anything that might come up. There are two reasons to do this. First of all, it gives them an opportunity to explain any potential yellow or red flags. Also, more importantly, background checks don't always catch everything. This way, they could shed light on something the background check might miss. There are several providers out there, but we use TLOxp® (www.tlo.com).

As mentioned at the beginning of this section, this list only barely scratches the surface of the extensive, serious work we put into operator due diligence at Asym Capital. If you want to learn more about conducting due diligence on an operating partner, we discuss this topic at length in the CFC Mentorship Program, our coaching program for real estate entrepreneurs who are just getting started in this industry.

For more information, visit www.cfcmentorshipprogram.com.

OUTSOURCING VS. PARTNERING

As a good friend and mentor of mine, David Coe, often says, "There is no 'I' in real estate. It's a team sport." Partnerships are the name of the game. However, you should always proceed with caution.

Real estate investments are illiquid investments in real property, typically with a hold period of five to 10 years. So, you have to be extremely careful about whom you choose as a partner and under what terms that partnership will operate. Keep in mind that the legal system is incredibly burdensome and costly, so dissolving an undesirable partnership arrangement can devastate your bank account, as well as your productivity and psyche.

How do you navigate this potential challenge while still benefiting from working with others? Here is the key: Although investing is a team sport, it does not mean that you need to bring on a partner who has the same amount of control as you.

I would suggest partnering with others who can add significant value to your firm as frequently as possible, but try to avoid locking yourself into a formal 50/50 partnership unless it's absolutely necessary.

It's also critical that you choose your partners strategically. Focus on partnering with or hiring individuals who enhance your strengths and supplement areas in which you may be lacking. Like most, I have many weaknesses and a few strengths. After years of working on projects with some extremely high performers in the real estate sector, I've found that one of my very few natural strengths is my speed of execution and implementation, the second KMI mentioned earlier. As soon as I come up with a good idea, I take action and don't stop until it's finished. Virtually all of my accomplishments in the real estate sector were completed at a pace at which most other people simply don't operate.

When working with other firms, my speed of implementation frequently gets bogged down if a key decision-maker is not as dedicated to accomplishing their goals in a short amount of time. This eliminates one of my core strengths and is one of the reasons I try to avoid allowing other individuals, or companies, to control the speed at which main benchmarks are hit.

This doesn't mean that I try to do everything myself—far from it. There's a categorical difference between hiring employees or contract workers and bringing on a partner who has managerial control over key decisions, such as when a project should be considered "finalized."

UNIQUE ABILITY®

Dan Sullivan is the creator of Strategic Coach®, a business coaching program for growth-minded entrepreneurs. Many of my favorite books about entrepreneurship were heavily influenced by Dan Sullivan and his life's work. Sullivan coined the term Unique Ability®, and it's one of the most powerful concepts to which I've ever been exposed.

Before deciding whether or not you need a partner or just need to outsource specific tasks, it's important for you to first take inventory of your natural strengths in an effort to identify your Unique Ability.

Here are a few components that make up your Unique Ability:

- Skills that have always come naturally to you
- Tasks that you absolutely love completing
- Skills or tasks that your friends and colleagues constantly compliment you on and ask you about
- Tasks that, when you complete them, bring significant value to others
- Tasks that you would complete regardless of how much money you had in your bank account

For reference, my most pronounced Unique Ability is communicating complicated real estate concepts effectively in a manner that educates and inspires both new investors and seasoned professionals alike. Additionally, I have a knack for identifying a compelling angle about a topic and explaining it in a way that entices the right clients. This is one of the reasons I decided to author this book and why I host a bi-weekly podcast.

The key here is that when you're looking for a partner, don't look for someone who brings the same thing to the table that you do. The division of labor is one of the most important concepts in all of human history and ingenuity and has created all of the benefits of modern society that we love and enjoy. I encourage you to tap into this concept and experience similar benefits within your firm.

Unfortunately, the education system often teaches us to focus on our weaknesses, which is antithetic to this incredible economic tool. If your report card came back with an A in science and a C in art class, teachers and parents may suggest you spend more time focusing on art. What's worse is that you'll get in a lot of trouble if you hire someone to do your artwork for you! In the marketplace, however, paying someone to "do your artwork for you" is an excellent strategy. In fact, the more you focus on your strengths, particularly within your Unique Ability, the less time you'll waste doing things you're less skilled at. Once you adapt to this mindset, you'll see your business scale quickly and effectively.

Once you've identified your Unique Ability, it's time to outsource virtually everything else. There is an abundance of websites and platforms to help you outsource the tasks that aren't your Unique Ability, but I've had the most success with Upwork (www.upwork.com). Like many outsourcing websites, Upwork has thousands of contract workers waiting to take tasks off your plate, all with different skill sets and hourly rates. Take your time when selecting who you work with, clearly outline the task at hand, and expect to get the quality of work you pay for. Navigating these sites is a critical skill for real estate entrepreneurs, and the earlier you get started, the better.

The more time spent working within your Unique Ability, the faster your business will scale, the more enjoyable your job will be, and the more you can work without experiencing burn out. However, just because a task is within your Unique Ability does not mean your career as a real estate professional will be easy. The strategy behind removing the tasks you are least competent in from your day-to-day is so you can focus on becoming an absolute master in your Unique Ability. This takes constant analysis, self-reflection, third-party accountability, and focus, along with many other traits I'll discuss later in this book. Don't think of concentrating on your strengths as the easy way out, far from it. The idea here is that the ROI that can be generated by challenging yourself to master your Unique Ability will produce far more efficient and lucrative results than struggling to work through your weaknesses. If you want to learn more about Unique Ability, I suggest you visit www.strategiccoach.com.

CHAPTER 5

Deal Structures for Real Estate Investments, SEC Exemptions, and Legal Documents

've raised capital for, and invested in, virtually every type of real estate structure that exists. They each have their pros and cons. In this chapter, I'll start by briefly summarizing the main ways, other than syndications, that people raise private capital for real estate transactions. Then, I'll go deep into the world of syndicated real estate investments, which necessitates a conversation on securities law, SEC exemptions, and legal documents. I made my best effort to provide enough context so that you can be a knowledgeable capital raiser, while still keeping the content digestible. With that said, this book is by no means intended to give you legal advice. You should always consult an attorney before raising money from anyone.

KEEP IT SIMPLE THROUGH REAL ESTATE DEBT INSTRUMENTS

One of the most straightforward ways to raise capital for real estate deals is to create a private debt instrument, which essentially is an IOU that grants an investor a pre-determined rate of interest. Of course, the lender will feel much more comfortable if the debt instrument is secured by something valuable, so most capital raisers will use an investment property as collateral in this scenario. You may have heard the term "hard money loan," which refers to debt collateralized by a "hard" asset, the most common being real estate. However, because the debt instrument is a private agreement between two parties, the collateral of a loan can be anything that's agreed upon, including a car, personal property, or even another IOU.

Here's a simple example of how this could work: Let's say you're a house flipper and have identified an investment property that will likely yield a 24% annual rate of return if completed correctly. If you borrow money from an investor at an annual rate of 8% to complete the flip and your investment plays out as projected, you'd be able to achieve an annual spread of 16% between the investment returns and the interest of the loan. Receiving a spread between the rate at which you're invested and the interest rate at which you're borrowing is referred to as "arbitrage," and it's one of the most popular ways to make money in the real estate sector. In this situation, rather than putting up all of the money for the flip yourself, you'd raise capital from an investor as debt and be the benefactor of this arbitrage opportunity.

Rasing Capital as Debt

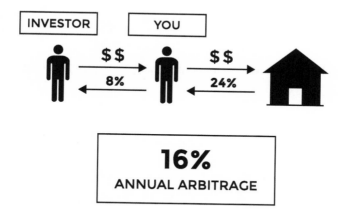

Main Benefits of Raising Capital as Debt

1. Most private loans can be created with low startup costs. While it's suggested that you have your counsel draft the documents of the loan, the attorney fees should be relatively affordable, given that the transaction is fairly straightforward.

2. The simplicity of the investment allows you to raise capital without hours and hours spent explaining the investment's structure to an interested party.

3. The loan investor/lender enjoys a predictable return with added protection from fluctuations in the market or the business plan's execution. For example, let's say you create a loan agreement and promise to pay the lender 8% interest. If you renovate the property but can't find a buyer who

will pay as high of a price as you originally anticipated, you still owe the lender his 8% interest rate. Many investors will find this desirable, which will make raising money as debt much easier for you.

Major Drawbacks of Raising Capital as Debt

1. You may be limited to having only one single investor per debt instrument. Without getting too technical, this is because having multiple investors on one note or loan, without all of the individual investors/lenders having control, could result in that loan inching closer to resembling a "security" (more on this later). This is a very nuanced area and, again, you should always consult an attorney when attempting to structure any deal like this. Suffice it to say, however, that the main challenge here is a lack of scalability. To create a new deal for each investor, rather than one large deal for multiple investors, your efficiency decreases and overhead increases.

2. As an extension of #1 above, since there's typically only one investor per note, unless that one investor happens to have millions to invest in a single investment, you'll likely be limited to the single-family sector.

3. Technically, you can create a debt instrument with whatever terms you like, but typically, real estate–backed debt is relatively short term (6-18 months). This means that you, as a real estate entrepreneur and capital raiser, will constantly have to find new projects to keep your investor's capital invested, which can be quite burdensome.

4. A debt investment is not an investment in actual property, so the investor you're raising capital from will not receive the tax benefits of owning real estate, such as depreciation. Interest received from investments in debt will be taxed at the investor's income tax rate, which can have a significant effect on their net result.

Speaking as an investor, debt instruments are great vehicles that anyone interested in diversification should have some exposure to. However, as a real estate entrepreneur, it's my perspective that the structure's limitations are significant enough to make other options more favorable. There are massive, extremely successful real estate firms that focus exclusively on raising capital as debt, but I strongly prefer to raise capital for equity ownership of physical property rather than simply having investors lend money for my purchases. There are many reasons for this, but the most important to me is that if I'm raising money from an investor, I'd strongly prefer to be investing alongside them, as opposed to simply borrowing money from them. This is important from an incentive alignment perspective, which I'll discuss in more detail in Chapter 10: Communicating to Attract and Influence Investors.

LEVERAGING PARTNERSHIPS THROUGH JOINT VENTURES

If you're working with one or more investors who want a more active role in the implementation of the business plan, a joint venture (JV) partnership is usually the best way to go. A JV is a structure in which two or more entities complete a project, and all parties have at least some amount of decision-making control regarding the business plan.

Joint Venture

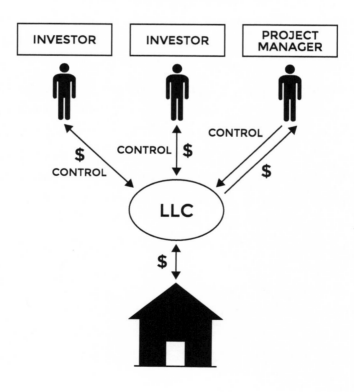

Main Benefits of Joint Venture Partnerships

1. While slightly more complicated than an IOU, the startup costs of a JV partnership will usually be limited to the creation and maintenance of a limited liability company (LLC) and the drafting of an operating agreement outlining how the business operates.
2. The structure allows you to rely on several partners, all of whom can bring different strengths to the table.
3. JV partnerships are a very common and straightforward investment structure. This drastically shortens the learning curve for potential investors and partners.

Major Drawbacks of Joint Ventures

1. Similar to any non-securitized investment, the most significant drawback is the lack of scalability. Unlike a debt instrument, JV partnerships allow you to have several investment partners. However, all of them have to be involved, at least to some extent, in the project. In these partnerships, the investors can't just invest and defer to an operating partner to make all of the decisions. If they do, they're slowly starting to edge closer to becoming a passive investor in a security, which I'll discuss momentarily.
2. Because the JV partners all have at least some amount of oversight and control, typically each JV participant is subject to the project's liability and debt obligations. Of course, there are exceptions to every rule, but this is the general rule of thumb.

3. Having multiple decision-making parties involved has the potential to increase the likelihood of a significant disagreement arising between the partners and can also reduce the speed at which challenging situations can be handled. There are ways to mitigate these risks, but the reality is without one key decision-maker who's primarily relied on, it can frequently become difficult to resolve matters quickly within this structure.

RAISING CAPITAL FOR SYNDICATIONS

If you've read a single article I've ever written, listened to a podcast I've hosted or appeared on, or even just know who I am, you probably already know that I'm a huge proponent of investing in and raising capital for real estate syndications. Syndications changed my life in such a monumental way that I'm not sure I'd be in my current position had I not discovered them early in my career.

A syndication is an investment structure in which several investors pool their capital together and invest in projects much larger than they could individually. These types of opportunities are frequently structured as LLCs and contain at least two classes of ownership shares: general partnership (GP) shares owned by the operating partner(s) and limited partnership (LP) shares owned by the passive investor(s).

Real Estate Syndications

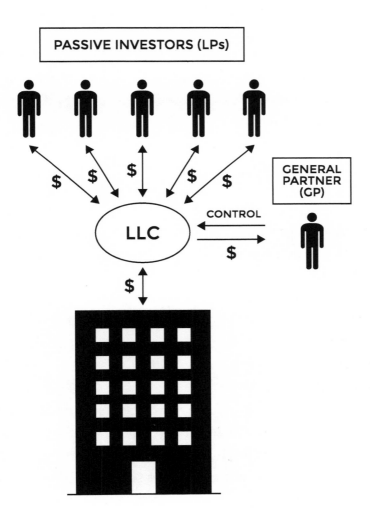

The delineation between the two shares is a critical part of this structure because it's one of the reasons investments in syndications are typically considered "securities." There are significant implications for dealing with securities, including more stringent requirements from the U.S. Securities and Exchange Commission's (SEC) formal guidelines and more dire penalties for disobeying their regulations.

So, what's a security? There tends to be a lot of confusion on this topic, but generally speaking, there's a simple test that can answer the question. This test is called the Howey Test, which is named in reference to the 1946 Supreme Court case *SEC v. W. J. Howey Co.*

Here are the four components of the test:

1. There's an investment of money.
2. There's an expectation of profit.
3. The investment of money is intended for a common enterprise.
4. Any profit comes from the efforts of a promoter or a third party and not from the efforts of the investors.

In short, if you're accepting capital pooled from investors who intend to receive a return on their investment but who will not have significant control or oversight of the asset's management, you're likely creating a security and, therefore, need to act in accordance with the SEC's guidelines on the topic. Since this is the exact outline of most syndicated real estate investments, understanding and acting in alignment with the SEC's rules is critical to your long-term success as a real estate entrepreneur.

These guidelines can be very challenging to navigate, so ensure that you're always working with a reputable attorney who has an in-depth understanding of securities law. Additionally, don't forget that the SEC regulates this matter on a federal level, but you must stay within state-specific laws and regulations surrounding securities as well. Furthermore, it's very common for real estate business to be conducted across state lines, so it's absolutely imperative that your counsel has a thorough grasp on the securities laws related to your state and whatever state(s) you're conducting business in.

MAIN EXEMPTIONS FOR REGISTERING SECURITIES WITH THE SEC

In the U.S., under the Securities Act of 1933, any offer to sell securities must be either registered with the SEC or meet certain requirements for exemption from registration. Registering with the SEC (typically referred to as "going public") entails extremely high upfront costs and ongoing reporting requirements that are too burdensome for most real estate deals. Because the economic and regulatory burdens of registering with the SEC would make most real estate offerings economically unviable, most syndication operators avoid this through an exemption from registration.

The most common exemptions from registering with the SEC are through either 506(b) or 506(c) of Regulation D (Reg D). Let's review the following chart from BiggerPockets to help understand which is best for you and your firm.

A Comparison of Offerings 506(b) & 506(c) Under Regulation D[4]

Item	506(b)	506(c)
Permitted Investors	Unlimited number of accredited investors Up to 35 non-accredited investors, who must meet sophisticated requirements	Unlimited number of accredited investors only
Accredited Verification	Issuer can rely on self-certification by each individual investor	Issuer must take reasonable steps to verify the accredited status of each investor Third party verfication is both recommended and common
Advertising Restrictions	Issuer may not advertise the offering Offering may only be presented by the issuer to prospective investors with whom the issuer has a sub-stantive pre-existing relationship	Issuer may advertise in any way that they want No substantive pre-existing relationship with prospective investors required.
Raise/ Investment Limits	No limit on either the amount the issuer can raise nor the amount each investor can invest	No limit on either the amount the issuer can raise nor the amount each investor can invest
Disclosure Requirements	Issuer decides what information to provide to accredited investors, so long as said information does not violate antifraud prohibitions Issuer must be available to answer questions from prospec-tive investors Issuer must make available to non-accredited investors the same information that they have provided to accredited investors	Issuer decides what information to provide to accredited investors, so long as said information does not violate antifraud prohibitions Issuer must be available to answer questions from prospec-tive investors
Filing Requirements	Issuer is not required to register with the SEC Issuer must file a Form D** to the SEC	Issuer is not required to register with the SEC Issuer must file a Form D** to the SEC

4 www.biggerpockets.com/member-blogs/10191/72197-private-placements-506-b-vs-506-c

There are several formal differences between 506(b) and 506(c), but from a functional standpoint, the most critical differences are regarding general solicitation and the steps required to verify if an investor is in fact accredited. We'll focus on these two aspects and how the decision between 506(b) and 506(c) could impact your workflow.

THE 506(B) EXEMPTION AND GENERAL SOLICITATION

Prior to 2012, Rule 506(b) (formerly "Rule 506") was generally considered the only viable option for exemption from registering with the SEC for most real estate syndicators. The exemption has many requirements, but one of the most important is that the issuer of the security is prohibited from conducting "general solicitation" or "general advertising" in its fundraising (i.e., no public marketing of the capital raise is allowed to occur). The easiest and most effective way to abide by the no general solicitation rule and be in compliance with applicable securities laws is to only raise funds from parties that the issuer has a pre-existing relationship with. This requires that each investor who's solicited by the issuer for a 506(b) raise be known to the issuer prior to receiving an offer to invest.

While the SEC hasn't drawn a line in the sand as to what defines a "pre-existing relationship," the commission has suggested that, among other things, the required relationship exists when an issuer knows enough about a potential investor to understand the investor's financial situation and has a record-keeping system in place to show that their relationship had been established prior to making them an offer to invest.

Generally speaking, the industry has interpreted non-action letters and other guidance from the SEC to be that an issuer would be advised to impose a "cooling-off" period of at least 30 days between the time when the substantive relationship is first established and an "offer" is communicated to a prospective investor.

In order to stay within these guidelines, here's a typical workflow an issuer would follow when conducting a 506(b) raise:

1. An issuer publicly advertises for their company but can't discuss the specifics of a particular opportunity.
2. An investor becomes aware of the company and enters their information into the issuer's database, whether online or through an initial in-person meeting.
3. The investor confirms they're an accredited investor as defined by the SEC, and the issuer keeps a record of this confirmation.
    a. An accredited investor is either a single investor who made $200,000 in the previous two years, a married couple who has cumulatively made $300,000 in the previous two years, or a person or married couple that has a net worth of $1,000,000, not including their primary residence.
    b. An entity such as an LLC or a corporation may be accredited if it has assets in excess of $5,000,000 or if all of the entity owners are accredited investors individually.
4. The issuer schedules a 30-minute phone call with the potential investor to reconfirm their accredited status by discussing

and asking questions about their previous experience in the real estate sector, their level of sophistication, and their investment history. Take note that throughout steps 1-4, no discussion regarding any particular investment opportunity has taken place.

5. 30 days after the investor has initially entered their information, they're able to view and invest in investment offerings. This period is the "cooling-off period" referenced above. During this time, investors have the opportunity to conduct additional due diligence on the issuing firm, so when it comes time to review and potentially invest in a specific investment, they'll have had plenty of time to get a thorough understanding of the company itself, as opposed to being introduced to a firm and then immediately feeling pressured to invest.

6. When an investor signs the legal documents to invest in the offering, they'll "self-verify" their status as an accredited investor by simply checking a box that states that they're in fact accredited.

As previously mentioned, please note that this is simply the industry-standard workflow for 506(b) offerings at the time of writing this book, and the SEC has intentionally left much of the language open for interpretation. Please don't take this as legal advice, as I'm simply reporting how most firms, in my experience, operate when claiming the 506(b) exemption.

Remember: If you're pursuing the 506(b) exemption, you can still publicly advertise for your business, but you're not permitted to advertise the details of a *specific deal* until a pre-existing relationship has been established with a specific investor.

ADDITIONAL SCRUTINY AND ADDITIONAL BENEFITS WITH THE 506(C) EXEMPTION

One of the most significant shifts in the business of raising capital took place when the JOBS Act of 2012 was signed into law. The passage of the Act had several significant implications for the financial sector, but in terms of this book, one ensuing change was that the legislation made it legal for companies to market their securitized real estate offerings to the public, giving many people access to real estate investments for the first time. This is the substantial difference between offerings under Rule 506(b) and Rule 506(c), the latter of which permits general solicitation.

However, the freedom to publicly solicit investors comes with additional burdens on the issuer of the security. Most notably, it includes the requirement that the issuer must take reasonable steps to confirm each of the investors' accredited status. Typically, most firms pursuing this exemption require that potential investors provide a third-party verification letter confirming the potential investor meets the accredited requirements. This letter can be completed by a CPA, broker-dealer, attorney, SEC-registered investment advisor, or third-party vendor (see next section). If the financial professional or attorney isn't already intimately aware of the investor's status, the investor will be required to provide proof of their financial situation through the provision of their income statements, bank accounts, stock and/or real estate portfolio, or proof of ownership of other assets.

Here's what a typical workflow might look like for an issuer of a 506(c) offering:

1. An issuer discusses the specifics of an offering to the general public on a publicly available webinar, podcast, social media platform, newsletter, advertisement, et cetera.
2. An investor visits the website of the issuer and self-verifies that they're accredited in order to access the offering documents.
3. As soon as the investor self-verifies their accredited status, they can instantly access the offering documents for a specific investment opportunity, including the legal documents.
4. After the legal documents have been reviewed and executed by the investor, they send them back to the issuer, along with a third-party verification letter that confirms their status as an accredited investor.
5. Once the third-party form has been reviewed and accepted by the issuer, the investor can fund their committed investment amount and be formally accepted into the offering.

As you can see, this process has the potential to be much more streamlined. Essentially, investors can almost instantly access the offering documents, as opposed to scheduling an introductory call and going through the 30-day cooling-off period prior to investing. This can significantly impact the likelihood of an investor moving forward with an investment, as many obstacles may arise within that 30-day time span. Furthermore, many accredited investors are busy individuals who may not have the time to reconvene with an issuer once their waiting period is up.

EVOLUTION OF 506(C)

When we first started Asym Capital, the industry had not yet responded to the inclusion of the 506(c) exemption and its respective requirements. Early on, many conversations with industry leaders, including representatives at some of the leading crowdfunding portals in the U.S., led me to believe that the ratification of 506(c) wouldn't significantly impact the industry as a whole. That conversation has shifted, and times have changed. I'm now a huge advocate of the 506(c) exemption, and we've moved towards exclusively pursuing 506(c) offerings at Asym Capital.

Why have we made this move towards 506(c) opportunities?

1. **With a 506(c) offering, I can discuss an opportunity on our podcast without worry of being in violation of the 506(b) guidelines that prohibit general solicitation.**

2. **While it's true that the third-party verification required to complete a 506(c) raise can cause some headaches, third-party vendors that provide this service are now readily available and have significantly streamlined this process.** For example, Verify Investor (www.verifyinvestor.com) and FundAmerica (www.fundamerica.com) offer this service and create easy-to-follow paper trails of third-party forms to protect you as an issuer. This way, you can automate receiving confirmation of each investor's status as an accredited investor, rather than complete the task yourself.

3. **With an increasing number of investors becoming accustomed to 506(c) offerings, it's now less burdensome to**

get investors through the third-party verification process. Several years ago, this process was quite challenging because it was often the first time investors had to compile their financial documents for a third party to confirm their status as an accredited investor. Once they've gone through the verification process, investors know exactly what to present the next time around, which streamlines the process.

All in all, issuers have much clearer guidelines for staying within the 506(c) exemption's requirements. It puts a spotlight on the extra level of scrutiny the issuer used to establish each investor's financial situation, and the gray area surrounding the definition of a "pre-existing relationship" is eliminated. Furthermore, it can free up an issuer to do media appearances without worrying that doing so may violate the general solicitation rules.

Even if you forgo general advertisement of your specific investment offerings, I still suggest considering the 506(c) route, as opposed to 506(b), given how much more certainty there is surrounding the rules of the exemption.

To further streamline the entire investment process, including the third-party verification step, we integrated our website with an investment portal that offers a full suite of services and tracks each investor's step as they make their investment, as well as all communications after the investment is made.

The investor portal is extremely costly, yes, but it's worth every penny, given the size and scope of our firm. It also alleviates many of the challenges associated with helping hundreds of investors through the multi-step process required by the 506(c) exemption.

Especially if you plan on raising more than $10,000,000, I suggest researching this type of portal, as it's one of the best investments we've ever made as a company. Not only does it reduce the administrative challenges associated with the investment process, but it also provides our investors with an institutional-quality reporting experience to a degree that was previously only available on mainstream brokerage accounts.

WHAT ABOUT NON-ACCREDITED INVESTORS?

The primary reason I chose this career path is to help people secure their financial future. I believe the way to do this is by getting money out of unpredictable, volatile investments like stocks and into predictable, cash-flowing assets like real estate. At first, my main goal was to help my friends and family invest, regardless of if they had a net worth of $5,000 or $5,000,000. In the early years, we created several 506(b) offerings and maxed out the allowed number of sophisticated, non-accredited investors in many of them.

Over time, I've learned it's much more favorable to deal exclusively with accredited investors. I get it: This isn't the best news, especially when you're just starting out. Every dollar counts, so excluding every non-accredited investor from your potential investment pool is a hard decision to make.

I have to break it to you, though: Non-accredited investors will invest the least, cause the most headaches, and, most importantly, are likely to invest far more than they should in your offering from a portfolio allocation standpoint.

We've been very fortunate in our investments' performances, but as with any real estate transaction, we take a chance on loss of principal each time we invest. In the event that something unforeseen does happen, we want to be certain that the investors are in a position to economically recover. The best way to ensure this is to only deal with accredited investors.

If you're still interested in helping your fellow non-accredited investors invest, I totally understand. The 506(b) exemption is likely a great option for you. In fact, if you're interested in focusing on the non-accredited investor niche, I suggest you research Regulation CF (Reg CF) and Regulation A+ (Reg A+), which are other exemptions for registering with the SEC that also allow non-accredited investors.

Neither of these additional options work for us at Asym Capital for a variety of reasons, but they might work for you and your business model.

It's worth reiterating that securities law is constantly in flux. The landscape of raising capital can change. Always consult with your attorney, as well as other successful real estate professionals in your network, prior to making a decision regarding this topic.

LEGAL ENTITY SELECTION AND CREATION

Disclaimer: Before setting up any legal entity, you should be confident that you're going to be able to raise capital. If you're just getting started and are unsure how much traction you'll have with potential investors, it might be wise to skip this section for now, read Chapter 6: Activating Your Investor Base, and implement

Raising Capital for Real Estate

the suggestions therein. If you complete the suggested action items in that chapter, you're sure to have some strong leads with investors before you formally open any legal entity and incur the fees associated with incorporating. Once you've gotten a few positive responses from potential investors, and it's clear you've created some interest in your business, come back to this chapter so you can learn about opening up your entity, as well as drafting its legal documents.

In order to ensure that your personal assets are not subject to liability related to your investment business, it's absolutely critical that you create, use, and properly maintain an entity that holds your ownership of the investment vehicles you create and raise capital for. While there are a number of different entities to choose from, for decades, the limited liability company (LLC) has been the preferred entity for real estate investors, due to its flexibility, reduced reporting requirements, and favorable tax implications. However, because there are a few options, always consult with your CPA and/or attorney prior to making a decision on this matter and, as always, please know that I'm not providing accounting or legal advice, nor am I advocating for any particular method.

To create an entity, you can have your attorney do it for you, or you can do it yourself on a site like LegalZoom (www.legalzoom. com). If you decide to go with the latter, be aware that there have been many instances where entities have been deemed invalid during court proceedings because they weren't set up correctly. In order to avoid such a potentially catastrophic nightmare, ensure that your attorney has reviewed everything so that you can be confident you're in good standing prior to doing business.

WHERE SHOULD YOUR LLC BE INCORPORATED?

While state-specific laws are constantly changing, the two states people most frequently use when creating syndications are Delaware and Wyoming.

Here are a few differentiating factors of each:

Benefits of Incorporating in Delaware:

1. Delaware provides the ability to functionally eliminate the fiduciary duties of the manager of the LLC with very few caveats. This provides an additional level of protection for the LLC's manager, which is especially important in the world of real estate investing.
2. Delaware permits series LLCs, which enable you to create multiple operating entities under the umbrella of a single LLC, with each entity being insulated from any liabilities that may occur with the others. (The case law on this matter is in its early stages, but it certainly looks promising.)
3. Despite the reality that maintaining a Delaware LLC is more expensive than its main competitor (see below), it's the most commonly used entity in the deals that we at Asym have raised capital for and invested in.

Benefits of Incorporating in Wyoming:

1. Wyoming provides the manager of the LLC with similar protections that Delaware does.
2. Creating and maintaining an LLC in Wyoming is considerably less expensive compared to Delaware.

3. Wyoming likely has the most favorable asset protection laws in the U.S., particularly as it relates to the case law surrounding its protection of single-member LLCs (LLCs with only one owner).

Since many real estate businesses are owned by one single individual, #3 in the above should not be overlooked. If you plan on being a one-person show, I suggest having your attorney specifically look into this topic prior to creating your structure.

If you're interested in learning more about Wyoming LLCs, check out E64 of the *Cash Flow Connections Real Estate Podcast*, "Why You Should Consider Using Wyoming for Your Next LLC."

As noted above, state-specific laws are constantly changing. It's always important to contact your attorney prior to creating your structure. Having said that, these two states have been the industry standard for several decades. It's likely they'll remain relevant to the "LLC location" conversation over the next several decades as well.

UNDERSTANDING, DRAFTING, AND EXPLAINING YOUR INVESTMENT'S LEGAL DOCUMENTS

Once you've created your entity and confirmed with an attorney that your structure will protect you and your assets, it's time to draft the legal documents that outline how business is to be conducted.

Before your eyes glaze over, I'll just come out and say it: The only people that get excited about drafting an operating agreement are the attorneys who are paid hundreds of dollars per hour to do so. However, if you're going to be successful in raising capital for real estate deals, it's absolutely critical that you understand the important components of the legal documents well enough to effectively discuss them with investors later down the road.

The purpose of this section is to provide you with a few important components of the legal documents that need particularly close attention, as they're the provisions that will most significantly impact the way the deal operates and are most likely to come up during due diligence calls with potential investors.

DIVING INTO THE OPERATING AGREEMENT

In Chapter 11, I'll provide you with my perspective on how to answer investors' questions about some of these topics. For now, just know these are the most important highlights to pay attention to when reviewing and drafting the opportunity's operating agreement:

1. **Summary of the business plan.** Ensure that your understanding of the summary of the business plan lines up with the actual verbiage in the operating agreement.
2. **Waterfall.** You should know the exact order by which the members of the LLC get paid. For example, a typical waterfall may include a preferred return to investors and a split between the GP(s) and the LP(s) above the preferred return.

3. **Distributions.** This section will outline how distributions are made, when they're required to be made, and under what circumstances the manager can decide to withhold distributions.

4. **Depreciation.** One of the many benefits of investing in real estate is the fact that, in a typical leveraged real estate investment, cash flow from operational income is usually tax-deferred, meaning there will likely be no tax due during the hold period. This is attributed to the benefits of depreciation, a tax write-off that accounts for the aging of the physical structure of the investment property. However, savvy investors understand that this depreciation tax benefit can be divided up between the LLC owners along whatever lines the operating agreement states, so it's important that you understand its division for your offering.

5. **Voting rights.** Investors want to know the circumstances under which they'll be able to vote and what percentage of the vote is required for certain non-day-to-day actions, like selling the property, replacing the manager, and accepting additional capital investments.

6. **Additional capital requirements.** You'll likely get more questions about this provision than any other, and for good reason. It's critical to have a clearly defined outline of: how it's determined that additional capital is needed; whether or not additional capital above the investors' original investment amount can be required; the penalty or penalties incurred if they don't contribute; and how additional capital that's not provided by investors, but is still deemed necessary, would be accepted into the offering.

7. **Transferability of shares.** Despite the fact that these investments should be considered "non-transferrable," your operating agreement should clearly outline how shares can be transferred in the event of an emergency and how to remedy the situation if need be.

8. **Reporting.** Ensure that the reporting schedule is clearly outlined in the operating agreement and that you're familiar with it so investors know they can rely on predictable communication after their investment has been made.

9. **Liquidation.** Once the business plan has been implemented, it will be time to sell the asset(s). Be certain that you're knowledgeable about how the operating agreement outlines the investment's dissolution, including the anticipated length of time, whether or not LP investors will have the opportunity to vote on the sale, and other matters surrounding how this will be handled.

Reading through legal jargon is most likely not the reason you got into the business of real estate. However, once you review a few operating agreements in detail (and especially once you help your attorney draft an operating agreement for your first deal), reviewing the important sections and getting a thorough grasp of how business is going to be conducted will be somewhat of a breeze. Plus, your ability to communicate to investors in the future, as well as your level of comfort with the material and your overall credibility, will increase exponentially.

SHOULD YOU CREATE A PRIVATE PLACEMENT MEMORANDUM OR JUST AN OPERATING AGREEMENT?

When it comes to investing in and raising capital for syndicated investments, one of the most daunting parts of the process is drafting a private placement memorandum (PPM). A PPM is an extremely dense and lengthy risk-disclosure document that includes the offering's operating agreement, as well as numerous other sections that are mostly designed to disclose information to the investor and better protect the issuer. Due to the intricacies of each investment and the level of detail each PPM needs to cover, having an experienced attorney draft a PPM from scratch can cost anywhere from $15,000 to $35,000.

While drafting a full PPM is certainly preferable because of the increased level of protection it provides the issuer, it may not be economically viable if you're just getting started and only expect to raise a few hundred thousand dollars.

The question becomes this: When is it appropriate to only provide investors with an in-depth operating agreement that costs somewhere around $5,000, as opposed to drafting a full PPM that could run upwards of $35,000?

I've discussed this topic at length with a variety of securities attorneys, and there's no set-in-stone answer to this question— but there are two important factors to consider. First of all, once your sphere of investors starts to get further and further away from your friends and family, the likelihood that you'll face some sort of legal challenge increases proportionally. Secondly, once you raise a considerable amount of equity, the overall deal size is large enough that a $35,000 upfront fee won't significantly deteriorate the return profile of the offering. From my perspective, if you're raising more than $500,000, or are raising capital from more than 10 investors, it's both economically viable and prudent to have your attorney draft a full PPM.

The numbers outlined above make sense for a variety of reasons, and many attorneys would agree that somewhere near those two benchmarks is a point at which it would be unwise to raise capital without a full PPM. However, as with anything in this book, don't take this as legal advice and check with your attorney.

CHAPTER 6

Activating Your Investor Base

N ow that your legal documents have been created, it's time to start raising cold hard cash.

This book began with a story about me falling on my face with a capital raise attempt through extended friends and family. However, as an investor looking for asymmetric outcomes, the risk-return ratio of that luncheon was incredibly favorable. The cost to me was minimal and could've resulted in a massive win for me and my company. It didn't turn out that way, but other than the emotional challenge I went through, there was basically zero downside.

This is why I'm a huge advocate for starting your investor outreach with your friends and family. After all, they already know and trust you and are likely interested in what you are working on. Additionally, there are no better people to practice your pitch on than those who will still like you, no matter what.

Make sense? Good. Let's get started.

In general, when I'm in the middle of a book-reading session, I dislike when the author requests that I complete some action item. I always skip over it because I'm clearly in the mood to read information, not do work-related tasks. I won't ask you to stop what you're doing right now and complete the task below. However, I'll ask you to quickly block out one hour in your calendar so you can complete the task first thing in the morning. Once you've put it in your calendar, get back to reading. We're just getting to the really good part.

To get the ball rolling with your initial outreach, complete a full export of your potential investor contacts to an Excel spreadsheet. This will help systematize your initial outreach process.

Here are a few suggested column headers for your Excel spreadsheet:

First Name	Last Name	Email	Phone Number

When you go through this process, include the following: all contacts made at the networking events you've been attending; people who might be interested in investing; people who probably wouldn't be interested but might know someone that could be; and any friends and family members who would appreciate insight into your work. If you have a few names that you'd like to include but are missing some of their information, don't hesitate to reach out to them directly or through someone who knows the needed information in order to completely fill the spreadsheet. For some readers, requesting this information from other sources might be a mental hurdle, but don't worry; you're not going to be spamming anyone. In fact, in the next section, I'll discuss how to position your first email to eliminate any of those fears by sending out an initial request that requires an opt-in before sending any investment opportunity.

INITIAL OUTREACH TO FRIENDS AND FAMILY

If you were able to complete your contact database chart and still have more time remaining in the one-hour block, you can go ahead and start drafting and sending initial emails. If, however, you spent the whole hour completing the contact form, schedule another one-hour block the following morning for part two of the task which is outlined below. Either way, ensure that you're intentionally scheduling and completing these tasks—and not trying to fit them into 15-minute breaks between phone calls and emails.

Once you have your time allocated and your contact list drafted, the next step is to take action and send out an initial email to each individual contact.

Here's an example outline of how the initial email should be structured:

Hey [insert first name],

I hope you're doing well. I wanted to let you know that I recently joined [insert company name] and will be working with them *on their next project. [Insert company name] is a real estate investment firm with more than 10 years of experience and $100,000,000 under management. Our main investment focus is on multi-family apartments, but we have experience investing in a variety of asset types. You can find out more about our firm here [insert link to website].*

There isn't an investment opportunity at this time, but are you interested in being on our investor list in the event we have a deal that fits our criteria? I won't be constantly emailing you, as we'll likely have three or four offerings this year.

Please let me know when convenient.

I like this email structure because it accomplishes five things:

1. **It establishes that you're working in the real estate sector.** In some cases, the reader might not be aware of this fact.
2. **It informs the reader about your partnership with an experienced team that already has a track record of success.** This way, the focus is not on your expertise, which could be limited at this time.
3. **It opens the door for conversation but doesn't put any pressure on the reader.** You made it clear there's no investment opportunity currently available. This is critical for alleviating your resistance to sending the email, as well as their resistance to responding!
4. **It shows that, while you're active in the market, highly desirable deals are rare and often unavailable.** This also gives the impression that you're in-the-know, which increases your credibility.

5. **It gives the reader agency to authorize you to send them future correspondence, rather than you simply signing them up for emails.** At this juncture, putting the ball in their court is a power move.

Let me guess: You have some serious initial aversions to sending these emails out. Are these some of the objections you have?

1. Your website isn't finished. *We'll get to that soon!*
2. Your email address ends in gmail.com as opposed to a business address. *Yep, that's coming shortly as well.*
3. You don't know the vocabulary of real estate well enough to hold a solid conversation with a potential lead. *If you reach out to them now, it will create some accountability for you to get through this book, at which point you'll understand a ton about communicating with investors.*
4. You have a few big fish that you think could really change your career and you don't want to approach them until everything in your system is perfect. *It's never going to be perfect. The most important ingredient for leveraging a key relationship like this is that you take action quickly.*

There are a million reasons why **not** to act now. Do you remember back in Chapter 3, when I mentioned the main traits mentors are looking for in potential mentees? Let's take a look at the first two Key Momentum Indicators (KMIs):

1. A sense of urgency to accomplish your goals
2. A high speed of execution and implementation

In order to strengthen these two KMIs *and* to confirm to yourself that you have what it takes, you **have** to act. Remember, it's not going to be comfortable from here on out, so you'd better get used to it. Just like with any muscle, it's one you have to train.

I've found that creating some external pressure and accountability is a powerful method for accomplishing major goals. For example, if you reach out to your inner circles and announce that you'll be contacting them soon with an opportunity, you significantly increase your accountability for taking action, consequently increasing the likelihood that you'll actually do so.

This modest request that you compose and send out a few emails comes at an intentional time, before I discuss creating a single piece of content (let alone building an entire brand). If you're not already in the habit of taking action, now's a great time to start. Don't simply skip over this advice and move on. Take five minutes right now to put time in your schedule tomorrow morning to make your Excel grid and send those emails. This is the first step in gaining the momentum you'll want (and eventually need).

SYSTEMS FOR HELPING YOUR FOLLOW UP

One reason people fall short in this business is that they have a weak strategy for following up with potential investors. Most people drastically underestimate the number of times required to contact a lead in order to get them to invest in an offering, and many capital raisers stop before the potential investor has even given their investment opportunity a second thought.

You're in luck, though, because I'm about to discuss some proven, efficient tools and strategies you can use to automate and systematize your follow-up communications with potential investors. Implementing the suggestions outlined below will allow you to create an automated and reliable process that will result in a much higher likelihood of capital being invested in the future.

In order to avoid the problems associated with haphazardly trying to remember who you met, who you should contact, and when you should contact them, it's absolutely critical that you integrate your communication system with a customer relationship management (CRM) software. There are myriad tools and apps out there to choose from, depending on the sophistication of your business and the limitations on your budget. However, you don't need to break the bank in order to implement something like this today.

Here are two tools we currently use at Asym Capital, as of the writing of this book:

1. **MixMax.** This is a software that amplifies Gmail capabilities, allowing you to complete a variety of productive, time-saving tasks within your email. The software allows you to send time-delayed emails, automate follow-ups, use templates to avoid re-writing emails, and share your availability for a call with one click.

2. **PipeDrive.** This is a CRM tool that focuses on sales management. It's extremely inexpensive compared to its competitors and very easy to learn. One of its greatest functions is that it doesn't allow you to omit a "next step" in your communication with the lead. This way, you're constantly

either moving the lead forward in the sales process, or you can remove them from the workflow (also known as a "pipe") if they end up passing. Follow-up reminders are an important aspect of the closing process because they give you the ability to rely on the automated system rather than cluttering up your headspace in an attempt to remember all of your contacts, your last communication with them, and the next time you need to follow up with them.

When used concurrently, these two tools (or their competitors) will immediately help systematize your follow-up process, which will become more and more important as you continue to grow your investor base. For example, if you use MixMax when you send out that initial email to friends and family, you could also pre-determine that the recipient should receive a follow-up message if they don't respond. For something like a cold request for an opt-in to your sales funnel, I would suggest sending only one follow-up email, which should read something like this:

[Insert first name],

I hope you're doing well. I wanted to follow up on this topic, as I know that emails can sometimes slip between the cracks. Would you be interested in receiving an update once we do have an investment opportunity available?
I look forward to hearing from you.

Thank you.

As you start to receive responses to either of these emails, start putting all of the "yes" responses into PipeDrive or a similar CRM tool so that you can track all communication from that point forward. This is the beginning of your investor list that will continue to grow for many years to come.

If you're unable to get a property under contract as anticipated, I recommend that you reconnect with the potential investor within no fewer than three months of them opting in, just to ensure them that you're still working in the business. When you reconnect, it's important to update them on your current focus points, even if it's just to explain why some of the deals you've been analyzing didn't work out. This is a great way to re-establish the connection and gain credibility, demonstrating how rare it is to come across deals that meet your specific investment criteria. It's critical that these leads don't go cold, so be sure to contact them at least every quarter with an update. After all, you already explained that you thought there would likely be only three or four offerings this year, so this is the frequency at which they anticipated you would contact them.

Another good item to include in this check-in email is the opportunity for people who are on your list to opt in to a more frequent rate of communication. In the next chapter, I'll discuss the types of content you can create so that you can contact them much more often without giving the impression that you're spamming them.

CHAPTER 7

Building a Brand
That Establishes Credibility

W hat would it take for you to wire $300,000 to someone you met online? When viewed through a certain lens, it's pretty remarkable that this could even happen at all. However, by the time you complete this book, you'll have a much deeper understanding of how you can position yourself to receive similarly sized wires from some of the savviest investors in the sector. This chapter in particular will examine some of the key strategies and tools you can utilize to create an infrastructure that allows investors to get so comfortable with you and your business, they'll eventually send you hundreds of thousands of dollars without so much as an in-person meeting.

As an example, we recently had someone sign up for our investment platform, confirm an investment amount, and sign the legal documents for a $300,000 investment, all within the same day. In fact, we didn't even speak to this investor on the phone through this entire process. How did this happen? No, it wasn't a glitch in the system. The investor was intimately familiar with our ethos, investment thesis, and reputation in the real estate arena. This was a result of years of work building our brand, creating thousands of sources of content, and establishing and maintaining our reputation of delivering for our investors. In fact, this particular investor was referred to us by one of our repeat investors, which is not at all surprising, given that they already felt very comfortable with us.

If this sounds like the type of streamlined system for raising investment capital you want to create, you have to architect an automated system for nurturing your leads through educational content and establishing credibility while doing so. From my perspective, this is the most efficient way to scale any real estate business.

What systems should you have in place to nurture these potential leads? You need a brand that investors know, respect, and trust. Let's start with Branding 101:

1. **Name.** I strongly suggest you choose a name that you can grow into over the next several decades. For example, if you're currently focusing on self-storage but may consider other asset classes in the future, avoid putting "self-storage" in your name. Or if the firm's name is your last name, what happens if you bring on a partner? I'm not saying you should avoid this, but it's just something to keep in mind. Take your time here, because you'll be stuck with it—and a surplus of branded swag—for a long time.

2. **Logo.** We've used 99 Designs (www.99designs.com) to provide all of our major logos (*Cash Flow Connections Real Estate Podcast*, CFC Mentorship Program, and Asym Capital). If you haven't used it yet, it's a crowd-sourced design resource that allows you to pick from hundreds of different designs while designers compete for your bid.

3. **Business cards.** Remember that whole part about avoiding the "business card spray-and-pray" strategy at networking events? With this same notion in mind, you should gladly spend more on 50-100 quality business cards than for 1,500 cheaply made ones. Sturdy, beautiful cards really stand out, and your goal should always be to have a memorable impact on a few people, rather than a forgettable impact on a lot of them. VistaPrint (www.vistaprint.com) and Moo (www.moo.com) are great options.

4. **Website.** We've always used WordPress (www.wordpress.com), though Wix (www.wix.com) is another viable option. This is the most important branding effort you'll undertake, but more on that soon.

5. **Business email.** Once you have your website URL set up, you can send emails from a business account. This adds a lot of credibility to all of your communications.

6. **Email signature.** Another nice and inexpensive touch is to have a beautiful, sleek, and branded email signature. Identify a few industry leaders that you respect and send those examples to a designer on Upwork as inspiration. They can code your proprietary design into your signature. Another option is to use New Old Stamp (www.newoldstamp.com), a site that will design and code your email signature for you.

7. **Social media.** Pick one or two social media platforms to focus on and post there at least twice per week. Right now, we're seeing the best results on Facebook and LinkedIn.

YOUR WEBSITE IS THE FACE OF YOUR COMPANY

If you plan on growing your real estate business quickly and efficiently, your website will likely be the most important component of your marketing efforts. Your website is your main storefront, billboard, and face of the company. It's not something to skimp on, so I'm going to add some additional details about what should be considered when developing it.

The best route to accomplish great things is to identify those who've already done great things and then implement their playbook, rather than trying to reinvent the wheel on your own. If you're considering developing a website or adding to your current one, I suggest dedicating at least one hour to exclusively reviewing some of your competitors' websites. Make note of how you think they addressed the list below and consider how you can tailor your website to the goals you're trying to achieve.

Here are a few important building blocks of a website, as well as some tips to develop them:

1. **Audience.** Consider your audience when creating your website's aesthetic and choosing the type of content you publish there. Before you get started, be conscious about the specific target demographic you're focusing on. This doesn't necessarily mean you need to be exclusively fixated on a

particular niche, just be cognizant of your primary audience. As an example, at Asym, we're focused on savvy investors who are often investing across several syndicators. They tend to listen to our podcast, in addition to many others, and are significantly more knowledgeable about the real estate sector than typical accredited investors because they've dedicated the time to become fluent in the language of the asset class. Because of that, our branding, articles, eBooks, podcasts, and the investments themselves are all tailored to a more sophisticated investor base. Our annual conference is titled the *Intelligent Investors Real Estate Conference* for a reason: We're intentional about keeping our branding consistent.

2. **Photography and videography.** Don't make the mistake of using copyrighted photos for your website! I inadvertently used some stock images for my first website without purchasing the rights to do so, which resulted in a $500 fine (negotiated down from $2,500). The way to avoid this is to purchase your photos from a company like Shutterstock (www.shutterstock.com). If you spend some time on Shutterstock, you'll likely see several photos or videos that you've seen elsewhere on the internet. Using photos that your audience has seen over and over again depreciates the content's authenticity because viewers know they aren't original. To mitigate the issue of different firms using the same photography and videography, Shutterstock released Offset (www.offset.com), an affiliated stock photography and videography company that only caters to high-end photos that aren't sold on such a massive scale.

High-caliber photography and videography are absolutely critical to your brand's appearance, so be sure to take the time to really find the visuals that work for you. If you don't have an eye for this, outsource the task to someone who does.

3. **Design and functionality.** You don't need your website to be overly complicated. It just needs to look amazing and work smoothly for a top-notch user experience. This is easier said than done, and you'll likely need to enlist help. In order to accomplish this without dedicating all of your time to learning how to design and code, hire an all-star graphic designer and webmaster. We have found ours on Upwork, but you can also ask for referrals or look to other outsourcing sites. You'd be surprised what you can get for $25-60 per hour from the pool of international talent.

4. **Call to action.** One area that deserves special focus is your website's call to action. This is the point in the website experience where a lead must provide their information in exchange for something they want. In the commercial real estate sector, the most powerful way to obtain a personal email is to give the viewer access to what they perceive to be high-quality investments or a high-quality piece of educational content. If there's no call to action, you'll never know who visited your site or if they enjoyed the content, and you won't be able to add them to that follow-up strategy of yours.

CREATING AN EDUCATIONAL CONTENT MACHINE

With the basics of your "storefront" in place, let's discuss your lead nurture system. The key to lead nurturing is constantly providing high-value content that your audience can truly benefit from. Positioning yourself as a thought leader in the real estate sector puts you on the fast-track to experience success in the business, particularly as it relates to your capital raising efforts.

There are many strategies to help you raise money for your real estate deals, but none are as efficient as creating a significant amount of educational content that aligns potential investors with your perspective on investing. The credibility you can establish by helping educate investors will further propel your career as more and more investors perceive you as a resource for quality information, if not a true thought leader in the sector. Additionally, throughout the process of creating this educational content, you'll come to understand your own business in much greater detail than before. This will amplify your expertise of the business and solidify your explanations of the most compelling points of a particular investment. Bonus: It doesn't require much of your time once the content has been created. Without a doubt, the combination of these factors will greatly increase your ability to raise investment capital.

Again, it's not simply about constant *contact*, it's about constant *content*. But how do you start? Just like you would with any significant project: time batch large tasks to improve efficiency and get the most done in the shortest time possible.

EFFICIENTLY CREATING 100 PIECES OF EDUCATIONAL CONTENT

You've already committed to creating this infrastructure, so the next step is to block out 60-180 minutes and write down at least 100 potential article topics related to real estate. Yes, you heard me correctly, *at least* 100.

Again, what are the two most important characteristics of a high performer? They have a sense of urgency for accomplishing their goals and a high speed of execution. The opposite also holds true; procrastination is the ultimate killer of success. If you can overcome this problem, you'll be head and shoulders above your competitors who struggle with it. The strategy behind creating more than 100 article topics is that most of the ideas you'll write down won't be worth a nickel and, therefore, knowing that you're going to create 100 of them completely removes the pressure to come up with something brilliant and drastically reduces the likelihood of procrastination. This way, you can burn through dozens of ideas without worrying that any particular article topic will make or break your career. Any strategy that will alleviate procrastination like this is usually a good bet but especially so when it comes to creative processes where it's so important to really let your creative energy just flow.

Here are five examples of article topics:

1. Investing passively versus actively
2. Five reasons self-storage will perform over the next five years
3. What interest rates really mean for housing

4. Recession indicators and what they tell us about the future

5. Should you be investing for cash flow or appreciation?

These examples are pretty darn good ideas, if I do say so myself. In fact, if you like them, use them! I'm sure your take on the topic would be different than mine anyway, so make those your first five ideas. Look, now you only have 95 to go.

Ensure that the topics are not time sensitive so any article-worthy concepts can remain evergreen on your website, and you won't have to go through this process again.

Once you've completed the task of creating 100 topics, I suggest putting them all in Excel and ranking them 0-10, with 10 being the highest quality, most aligned with your brand, and most compelling to your audience. Then, sort the articles in reverse numerical order, putting 10's at the top. The first 10 topics at the top of your Excel spreadsheet should be articles on your website.

It would be remiss of me to not mention search engine optimization (SEO), although I believe the actual content is much more important than keyword density. But it doesn't hurt to consult Google Keyword Planner to see which key phrases are actually searched the most. I wouldn't go so far as to cater the content around keywords because the quality of these articles should supersede the keywords you use, but it would be unwise to go through all this work without considering the keyword component.

Once you've established which topics you are going to cover, it's time to create some amazing articles. In order to write these articles as quickly as possible, I suggest time batching this task as well and establishing a recurring content creation schedule. For example, write from 7:30 a.m.-9:00 a.m. every Monday, Wednesday, and Friday, completing them one by one. Another option would be to solely write from 9:00 a.m.-2:00 p.m. every Thursday. Regularity will be key in completing this massive task as efficiently as possible, thus reducing procrastination and the cognitive fatigue associated with trying to spontaneously remember to write on certain days or randomly jotting down notes in between phone calls. Pick a schedule that works for you and stick to it.

When it comes to actually writing the articles, just let it flow. The first draft of these articles will likely be filled with mistakes, but turn off the parts of your brain that want to edit and perfect each word and commit to writing in a free-flowing manner. Burn through the words and once you've covered the topic adequately, you can go back, potentially with a copyeditor, and wordsmith what you wrote.

The completed articles should be 1,000-1,500 words, offering enough detail to establish your expertise in the space and educate your potential investors. During these head-down, three-coffees-deep work sessions, keep your particular audience top of mind when both brainstorming article topics and actually writing the content. When you can think like your audience, you'll have a much easier time talking to them. That way, the finished product will be a lot more appealing to your target demographic.

Once you've established the top 10 article topics, you still have 90 ideas left that you've already created. From those 90, there are likely 52 topics that can be used for outgoing email blasts. Why did I specifically choose 52? Because if you were to draft and send one of these emails out each week through a drip campaign, it would provide regular, informative content to a new investor for an entire year.

Emails should be shorter in length, roughly 300-500 words, and should be written with the intention of intriguing the readership. Don't be afraid to use bulleted lists when appropriate as opposed to paragraphs, so that time-sensitive readers can understand your points as quickly as possible. The goal of these emails should be to attract them back to your website, rather than make their heads spin with tons of data or long-winded explanations. If they want that extra level of detail, they'll need to read one of your articles on a related matter or one of your eBooks, which I'll address in the coming section.

We use Mailchimp (www.mailchimp.com) to facilitate our weekly email blasts, but there are other options like ActiveCampaign (www.activecampaign.com) or GetResponse (www.getresponse.com), all with different benefits and prices.

When I first launched Asym Capital, I took about one month to write all of the articles, and then I drafted 52 emails over a few short weeks. Because the articles are evergreen, some of them are still used to this day. In fact, people frequently comment or have questions regarding content I wrote years ago. This is one of the reasons why it's critical to ensure that the topics aren't time sensitive and can add value for the foreseeable future.

If you're first getting started, your understanding of the space will change significantly every three to six months, so my suggestion is that you put your strongest emails in front and switch out the weaker emails as you continue to learn, grow, and write new content. This way, any weak emails will continue to be pushed further and further down the list, so that no one actually ever reads them.

The beauty of creating a substantial amount of useful content in one fell swoop is that once it's done, you can switch cognitive gears to another task for several months, without worrying your leads are going to go cold due to lack of contact. Just be sure to set a reminder in three to six months and spruce up the drip campaign with the new ideas and topics you've learned since you first completed this task.

Now that you've created the content for 10 articles and 52 emails, what do you do with the remaining 38 topics? If you think there's something of substance left on the list, there's no reason for it to go to waste. Block out time to write short social media posts on any remaining topic you think might be interesting to your potential investors. By front-loading your content creation for everything from long-form articles to quick social media snippets, you're truly maximizing the time spent on the original 100-topic exercise.

EMAIL PREFERENCES

As technology evolves, email is becoming the most direct means of contacting busy professionals, even more so than their cell or business phones. (This is certainly true for me.) Because of this shift, email addresses need to be treated with the respect that they deserve. If a potential investor gives you their email address, give them the ability to adjust their preferences in accordance with the type of content they want to receive, as well as the frequency at which they want to receive it.

Before you subscribe them to every piece of content you create from now until the end of time, let them opt in or out of specific types of communication and select how often they want to receive emails. One way to do this is when a potential investor subscribes, they should be prompted to select the types of content that they would like to receive. Newsletters, articles, quarterly updates, and new investment offerings should all be separate campaigns. You can also allow subscribers to batch the communications weekly, monthly, or quarterly to avoid flooding their inbox. No one wants to be *that* guy. Sending too many emails, or emails that are irrelevant to the recipient, may cause them to resent it every time they see you crowding their inbox—or, worst of all, unsubscribe from your list.

This includes your list of friends and family that I discussed earlier. If you initially told them you would only contact them with new investments, make sure to request they opt in to other types of communication prior to sending them anything else.

Take this seriously. Your potential investors are the gateway to making all of your real estate dreams coming true. The last thing you want to do is to spam potential investors into hitting the unsubscribe button, and that's easy to avoid by providing the option to edit their email preferences.

THE EDUCATING, ENTICING EBOOK

When it comes to getting significant results efficiently, there's no better mechanism to educate investors than an eBook. They're free to distribute, can be jam-packed with information-rich content, and are an excellent way to supplement your emails and articles. They should be roughly 7,000-12,000 words in length and discuss a particular topic that directly aligns with your firm's investment strategy. At this length, it will take most people about 30-45 minutes to read and should provide enough insight to thoroughly analyze, defend, and justify your thesis of a particular investment or your strategy as a whole.

The easiest way to structure an eBook is in a numbered list format, for example, *10 Ways to X* or *10 Things You Need to Know About X*. In fact, the first eBook I ever authored was *Rest Easy Real Estate: 11 Ways to Avoid Investment Nightmares*. You can download it at www.raisingcapitalforrealestate.com.

Another eBook we had a lot of success with is *Little Boxes, Big Profits: A Passive Investor's Guide to Self-Storage*, which is available at www.raisingcapitalforrealestate.com.

Our Mailchimp account is connected to our website, so these eBooks are automatically delivered to potential investors when they sign up for our mailing list. In fact, we have sent these eBooks to thousands of investors without it taking any of my time or effort once the content has been created.

Here are a few suggestions for writing an eBook:

1. **Make a concerted effort to guarantee that the content will be valid and applicable to your company for years to come.**

While they're the gift that keeps on giving, eBooks do take time, thought, and effort up front, so you don't want to feel like you have to write 10,000 new words every six months.

2. **Include calls to action throughout the eBook that direct readers through the steps they should take if they're ready to invest.** Most books and eBooks are not read to completion, so don't wait until the very last minute to direct your readers to your investment opportunity. Keep in mind, your eBook is probably free, so don't feel uneasy about pitching.

3. **Take advantage of the additional word count by including some hard data, presented through charts and/or graphs to verify the claims you make.** Use data from objective third parties and provide sources so that readers can confirm the information's legitimacy if they choose to do so.

4. **Select a formatting structure that's easy on the eyes and grabs the reader's attention at the right time.** Again, since your eBook is most likely going to be free, many people will simply skim through the content. Use this to your advantage. Don't hesitate to use large headers above important paragraphs, bold fonts, and colored text to highlight the most compelling narratives. This way, skimmers will stop, read a few words, and make the decision of whether or not to continue. This can convert skimmers to readers and eventually turn them into investors.

5. **Like with everything you produce, your eBook should be beautiful from a design perspective.** Don't skimp out here.

Here are two added bonuses of writing an eBook:

1. **Having an educated and aligned investor base will significantly reduce the number of questions you'll have to answer during the due diligence process.** Investors may have questions about the specifics of a particular offering, but you likely will not need to explain the big-picture thesis of the asset class if they've already read your eBook on the topic. From a scalability standpoint, this makes a huge difference.

2. **Taking the time to solidify your understanding about the topic of your eBook will substantially help your ability to communicate to potential investors.** You'll be surprised at how much more thorough your thoughts are required to be when actually putting pen to paper. This will increase your level of knowledge on the topic, as well as your confidence, which investors will quickly pick up on.

To put it bluntly: Write an eBook if you want to be successful. Even in the worst-case scenario where you spend tons of time writing it and literally no one reads it, you still get bonus #2 above, which I'd bet will more than make up for the time you invested in the writing process.

In my experience, in terms of getting dollars invested in your offerings, there's no more efficient way to spend your time than creating and optimizing this infrastructure of educational content. There's very little risk due to minimal overhead costs, and the benefits that can be achieved, such as pre-emptively educating your investor base and improving your ability to communicate effectively, overwhelmingly make up for the time it takes to create the material.

THE POWER OF PODCASTS

From an influencer's perspective, nothing is more powerful than literally being plugged in to someone's ears, especially if you're talking about topics of interest to them. You can make a huge impact just by sharing ideas, but if the listeners actually implement what you're advocating, it may completely change their life's trajectory. Trust me, I know. I've received numerous emails and have had many conversations from people around the world who've entirely changed their perspective on a variety of topics and/or made significant investment decisions based on some of the conversations we've had on the *Cash Flow Connections Real Estate Podcast*.

As of the writing of this book, the podcast medium is experiencing one of the most rapid growth periods of any media outlet in history. To put things in perspective, iTunes had received a total of 7,000,000,000 downloads in 2014. By 2018, that number had skyrocketed to 50,000,000,000.[5]

However, this doesn't mean that the time to get involved in the world of podcasts has passed you by. In fact, nothing could be further from the truth. **There has never been a better time to get your message out to eager listeners, especially those who are**

---

5   www.9to5mac.com/2018/04/29/apple-podcasts-statistics

already interested in your perspective on various niche topics related to your real estate business.

Once you've created an eBook, the hard work is done. You've thought through a topic in enough detail to write out 10,000 words or so, and now you're ready to go on a podcast tour to share your thoughts and direct listeners back to your website where they can download your new eBook.

Here are a few steps to achieving podcast fame:

1. **Hire a virtual assistant (VA) on Upwork to make a list of 50 podcasts about real estate investing.** They can create this list by searching "real estate investing" in iTunes.
2. **Have your VA create a Google Sheet/Excel spreadsheet with the following headers in columns:**
    a. Name of the podcast
    b. Link to the podcast in iTunes
    c. Number of Twitter followers
    d. Number of comments in iTunes
    e. Host's email
    f. Podcast's alignment with your eBook topic (this could be a numeric value, such as 1-5)
3. **Once you have this spreadsheet, sort by whichever metric you think is most important.** From there, make a business decision regarding whom to contact first. If you're just starting out, I would begin with a combination of the most aligned and the least popular. (You'll thank me later.) This is the route that will most likely get you some momentum, as the less popular shows are more open to take a risk on a lesser-known guest. Furthermore, your first podcast

interview will probably be your worst, so you don't want to do it on a large stage. Additionally, once you have a few under your belt, the more popular shows are much more likely to have you on as a guest.

4. **Create a one-page "Speaker Highlight Reel" with your headshot, your bio, and a summary of the topics you would like to discuss on their show.** If you've already been a guest on other podcasts, include links to those. This will help save the podcast host a considerable amount of time.

5. **Make sure to listen to at least one recent episode of the show prior to reaching out.** This way, when you do initially contact the host, you can thank them for their recent interview and acknowledge a specific takeaway you appreciated from the previous guest or general topic.

6. **Reach out to the hosts directly—and don't outsource this to a marketing agency.** Due to the large number of people who are looking for speaking invitations on podcasts, hosts receive dozens of guest suggestions from marketers each day. Receiving these emails from an unknown marketing company is a little annoying, so take the extra time to reach out directly. You can have your VA contact podcast hosts via your email account but, given the line of work we're discussing here and the sensitive nature of the information investors will likely be sharing with you via email, this should probably be avoided. It doesn't take that long to send a handful of emails to a handful of hosts, so just commit and execute.

7. **Only send one follow-up email.** Look, I know it hurts to hear, but they received it the first time. The second email

is a nice reminder, and anything above that is a nuisance. Real estate is a massive sector, but it frequently feels like I know 15 people in the entire business, and word always gets around. If you send several follow-up emails, the receiver will never forget your name—and not in a good way.

8. **Always be cordial!** Remember that if you're pitching yourself as a potential guest, you're essentially trying to sell them on you. They don't owe you anything, including a response. If they don't think it would be a good fit, thank them for their time, wish them good luck with their program, and don't take it personally.

The strategy outlined above can be used for any news and media outlets, but I've found it to be particularly effective for the podcast medium. There's less bureaucracy with this form of media, given the simplicity of what's required to conduct a podcast, so it's likely that you only need to get through to one person in order to be a featured guest. Either way, this is an excellent way to spend your time, especially since you just wrote an eBook and should be extremely well prepared to discuss the topic at hand.

Podcast interviews are a strong source of credibility because they're intimate, compelling, and reusable. Unless the host decides to discontinue their program (which does happen), you'll be able to send these interviews to your network for years to come.

CHAPTER 8

Creating a Professional Executive Summary and Conducting Compelling Webinars

I f you've ever taken a cursory glance at the study of sales psychology, you probably know that people largely base their purchase decisions on emotion, rather than analytics, metrics, graphs, and data points. This is certainly the case in the investment world, and it's not just true of inexperienced investors. In fact, everyone from Main Street investors to Silicon Valley tech startups to multi-billion-dollar hedge funds all move forward with investments primarily because of the feelings they have about the opportunity, as opposed to logical analysis. Rather than try to fight this reality, we need to accept it, embrace it, and take it very seriously when it comes to anything we put in front of investors. At no time will this be more important than during the creation of your offering's Executive Summary (ES).

At its core, the ES is a business plan for the investment that outlines the strategy, summarizes the plan for implementation, justifies the thesis, and provides background on the key parties involved. It should be a given that the information provided in the ES will need to be top notch. These documents will be reviewed by high-income earners who are contemplating investing tens of thousands, even hundreds of thousands, of dollars with you. The language and the content should be appropriate for such an audience. Additionally, because many investors will judge an investment based on how professional the deck *appears* to be, you should consider the graphic design component of your ES as equally important to the content. Yes, it's true that there are many successful real estate firms that have been able to get away with offering documents with subpar graphic design, but the industry is changing, and there will be no excuse for anything but clean, beautiful Executive Summaries going forward.

STRUCTURE OF THE EXECUTIVE SUMMARY

While an ES can be organized in a variety of ways, you can find a typical layout of an ES below. Please note that, other than the Disclaimer section (which should always be first), this structure is flexible and should be adjusted based on a variety of factors, including your personal preference.

1. **Disclaimer.** Before getting into anything related to the investment, it's important to disclose that the ES is simply a pitch deck, and no investment can or should be made based on it

alone. Investments can only be made through review and execution of the Operating Agreement (and potentially the PPM). Feel free to review our standard disclosure at www.raisingcapitalforrealestate.com.

2. **Investment Overview.** In this portion of the ES, you should briefly explain the overview and objective of the investment. The idea is to get the main point across in the first few sentences. This chart or paragraph should explain the size of the raise, the location of the asset(s), and the background of the operating partners. I highly suggest including this outline in the Investment Overview, so even skimmers can quickly grasp the big picture without needing to read every word.

   a. **Asset Class**
   b. **Investment Strategy (development, value-add, stabilized, et cetera.)**
   c. **Equity Raise**
   d. **Hold Period**
   e. **Market**
   f. **Waterfall**
   g. **Annual Cash Flow**
   h. **Annualized Return**
   i. **Distribution Timing**
   j. **Minimum Investment**

3. **Strategy.** This section should be used to explain how the business plan will be executed. The goal is to specifically communicate how value will be created in the particular investment, as well as how to capitalize on that value creation. For example, if your strategy is to purchase mismanaged assets, raise

rents, decrease expenses, and sell, you should explain how you'll accomplish these goals here.

4. **Investment Thesis.** The purpose of this section is to communicate not only what makes the investment thesis so compelling but also why the investor should take action now. In this section, include economic and market data that urge potential investors to make a move, as opposed to waiting on the sidelines. If possible, include information about why other firms have not yet taken advantage of this opportunity but likely will soon. By doing so, you're driving this message home: Time is ticking, and the opportunity won't be around forever. Investors are more likely to pay attention when presented with a sense of urgency and, therefore, are more likely to move forward.

5. **Investment Highlights.** This section is usually another chart or bulleted list that reiterates the most persuasive components of the investment. For example, it should highlight the favorable market advantage provided by the background of the operating partner, the downside protection of the investment vehicle, the favorable waterfall for investors, and anything else you anticipate your investor base may find important or interesting. Many investors will skim the ES for information, and only stop to review the highlights. Use four to six bullets and make the case for the offering as concisely as possible.

6. **Financials.** The goal of this section is to provide the opportunity's financial projections and pro forma. Clearly outline how dollars flow from rental and ancillary incomes to the investors. One thing to highlight is the "key assumptions,"

which are the most important determiners of the offering's success. Of course, in other sections of the ES, you need to justify why each key assumption is conservative, achievable, and puts you in a position to deliver for your investors.

7. **FAQs.** In this section, you can preemptively provide answers to some of the most frequent questions investors ask. This section is critical because addressing the major questions upfront will both add credibility and reduce the amount of time you'll spend answering questions during the capital raising process. The goal for the FAQ section is to address functional and transactional questions, as opposed to specific due diligence–related questions, which usually require more explanation than appropriate for an ES. Here are a few examples of the types of questions to include in the FAQ section:

   a. **When does my preferred return start to accrue?**
   b. **When should I expect my first distribution?**
   c. **Can I invest through my self-directed IRA?**
   d. **Will the offering utilize debt financing?**
   e. **Can I sell my shares before the offering is liquidated?**

8. **Case Studies.** Include at least two case studies of offerings of a similar profile to the subject opportunity. This assures investors that you and your team have had success with the business plan, and the proof of concept has already been established. Including photos of these previous assets will increase your credibility, as a picture of a previously owned asset tells a much more enticing story than just text on paper.

9. **Meet the Team.** You don't have to provide your entire life story in the bio section but be sure to introduce yourself to

potential investors. Highlight the most important business accomplishments you and your key team members have achieved, particularly those closely related to the offering. Usually, 150-200 words on each key team member should allow you enough room to accomplish this goal.

You're not trying to overwhelm your passive investors with information here. Remember, most passive investors are not full-time real estate professionals. They're likely deferring to your expertise to a certain degree and don't need every detail you've learned through the pursuit of this particular investment offering. The objective is to provide them with enough relevant information, as succinctly as possible, so they can feel confident in their understanding of the business plan and decide if it's a good fit for them.

Unfortunately, many investors will not take the time to review every single word of the ES. Most of them will skim the content looking for the highlights. This is why it's absolutely critical to repeat the most important aspects of the investment several times throughout the document. Use bullet points, charts, and graphs whenever appropriate to ensure that those skimming the deck are made aware of the most compelling reasons to invest, while driving the point home for those reviewing the opportunity in detail.

In total, the deck should be no more than 20-25 pages. There's no reason to go overboard here. Quickly make your case for the investment, back up your claims, and paint an easy-to-understand picture as to why you're worth making a bet on. Our decks typically consist of 5,000–6,000 words, which is plenty of room to communicate to any passive investor why we think the investment deserves their attention and investment capital.

CREATING AND DESIGNING THE EXECUTIVE SUMMARY

Your ES needs to look nothing short of spectacular. This is why it's critical to hire an all-star graphic designer who can really make your offering deck stand out; it should be like love at first sight. If you're in the process of raising $1,000,000, don't be afraid to spend $1,000 on a pitch deck that has the ability to wow potential investors. Remember, $1,000 is just .01% of $1,000,000, so this is an efficient way to spend the money. Also $1,000 is just 1% of $100,000, so if just one investor moves forward because of the design quality of the ES, you'll likely have paid for the expense immediately. I emphasize this because I've seen many capital raisers who struggle to raise capital and never contemplate if the graphic design of their offering might be the cause.

When selecting a graphic designer for your job, only hire someone who can create decks in PowerPoint, Keynote, or another popular presentation software. This will streamline the process and reduce costs when it comes time to convert your ES to a live presentation.

If you're going to use images of the property, only use top-quality photographs taken by a professional photographer. You can hire a photographer on Thumbtack (www.thumbtack.com), which will give you access to photographers in virtually any city in the United States. The quality of the photos of the asset can make or break the appearance of the ES, so don't be afraid to spend $500-$1,000 on a photographer to really make the images pop. If you choose, you can also request they shoot video footage of the asset. We have had significant success using drone footage of several of our assets to showcase the quality of our properties and their surrounding areas.

You can get a great example of a beautifully designed ES by going to www.raisingcapitalforrealestate.com. Take note of the quality of the photos, text, sizing, font, and structure. If you simply mimic this structure and match the design to your brand's aesthetic, you should have a top-quality ES that will establish credibility and help you close the deal.

CONVERTING YOUR EXECUTIVE SUMMARY INTO A WEBINAR PRESENTATION

Once you've created the ES, it's time to use the original PowerPoint or Keynote file to give a webinar presentation to an online audience. This strategy allows potential investors to view the ES in a whole new light, one with the greater sensory input of a stimulating video, as opposed to text-heavy pages. You've already done all of the hard work creating the ES, and now you can reuse that content for another scalable platform.

During this webinar presentation, you'll simply go through the most important slides of your ES and discuss the main points over a 30-minute period. Before conducting your webinar, however, it's important that you make some crucial changes to your ES. If you chose a graphic designer who already works in PowerPoint or Keynote as suggested above, making these edits will be easy because these programs are designed for presentations.

Here are a few suggestions for reworking the Executive Summary for a webinar presentation:

1. **Unlike the structure of the ES, I would recommend beginning with a brief intro about who you are and your experience in the sector, immediately after the Disclaimer section (which should always be first).** Since you're speaking directly to an audience here, it's more natural to introduce yourself, rather than just jumping into the details of the investment offering.

2. **Each bullet point, or otherwise separated points, should be individually animated.** In order to keep your audience's attention, start each slide with a relatively blank screen, then pull up each bullet as you discuss each topic. This will focus your audience's attention on the points you're making when you're making them, as opposed to the audience reading ahead and tuning out after they think they already have everything they need to know. You don't want to draw attention to the animation itself though. (This means no "cartwheel in" or other elaborate animations.) Directional animations like a timeline slide that starts on the left and animates towards the right are particularly appealing for viewers.

3. **The presentation itself (excluding the Q&A) should be no more than 30 minutes.** Before turning the material over to your graphic designer, give the presentation a few times and see if you need to edit and remove some slides to stay

within the 30-minute limit. As discussed in *Pitch Anything* by Oren Klaff, people's attention spans are far less than what most people assume. If you haven't given someone all the information they need to decide if they are interested in the offering within 30 minutes, you're likely negatively impacting your ability to close (oh, and just wasting everyone's time).

4. **The last slide of the presentation should be a Q&A slide that includes your headshot and the branding of your company (header photo of your website, logo, or something similar).** This is a nice touch, as opposed to simply taking questions while a slide which is full of information is still up on the screen.

Once the ES has been converted to a dynamic presentation, it's time to drive traffic to your webinar and explain the benefits of the offering to interested investors.

Here are a few tips for conducting webinar presentations:

1. **Have a systematic process for handling invitations, RSVPs, and declines.** We like to use Eventbrite (www.eventbrite. com) to handle all of our invitations and RSVPs. The free version should provide you with all the bells and whistles you need. It doesn't require much on the attendee's part, so it's a win-win. The website also provides automated reminders that you can send out to potential attendees, which helps automate your pre-webinar promotional communications.

2. **Practice with mastery in mind.** There are enough unknowns in the world of real estate: Your ability to present effectively

should not be one of them. It's not enough to simply repeat the content over and over until you "know" it. In order to achieve mastery, record yourself giving the presentation and analyze it, take notes, and find ways to make it better, punchier, and more compelling. I've found that it also helps to give the presentation in front of someone to get over any performance jitters. Asking for feedback is always helpful as well.

3. **Make absolutely sure that the sound quality is top notch.** Fortunately, a few dollars go a long way here. For less than $150, you can pick up a microphone that will have you sounding like a pro in no time. One of the most popular and economic options is Blue Yetti USB Microphone, which retails for about $120 on Amazon. I also suggest purchasing a pop-filter to improve the listeners' experience by reducing the infamous "popping" of the microphone. You should also schedule a 15-minute sound check prior to the beginning of the webinar, so you can ensure the audio, video, and recording mechanisms are all working. If you decide to forgo making this investment, don't say I didn't warn you when every single comment about your webinar is regarding the sound quality.

4. **Encourage people to ask questions during the Q&A, but always have some good questions as backup if no one speaks up.** Even though there might be a considerable number of attendees, people may, for a variety of reasons, be reluctant to directly ask you questions. Because I've found the Q&A section to be a critical part of the webinar presentation, I recommend being prepared; in the event

no one speaks up, you can say something like "we actually have a few questions sent in via email," and jump right into your pre-written questions. If you're looking for examples, the FAQ section of your ES is a good place to start.

5. **After the webinar is completed, be sure to send out a link to the recorded version as soon as possible for those who weren't able to make it, as well as those who want to listen again.** Now that it has been recorded, your presentation should be forwarded within 24 hours of the webinar to anyone interested in the offering. Eventbrite makes sending an email to all invited parties very easy to complete, which is another bonus of the software.

6. **Regardless of whether or not you think someone has already reviewed the ES, always send them the recorded webinar.** Yes, the material is almost all the same, but some people learn better through presentations, rather than reading it themselves. Plus, the more times it's communicated, the more likely the information will sink in.

We currently use Zoom (www.zoom.us) for our webinars, which allows you to record the webinar, upload it to Vimeo (www.vimeo.com) or YouTube (www.youtube.com), and then send out a link to those who couldn't attend the live version.

If you're interested in an example of a presentation we made based on an ES we created, you can check out one of our recorded webinars at www.raisingcapitalforrealestate.com. This presentation led to an oversubscription of the offering very quickly, so using it as a template wouldn't be a bad idea.

CHAPTER 9

Hitting Investors Where It Counts

One of the reoccurring themes in this book is the importance of creating high-quality content and then reusing it for multiple purposes and across several media. This increases the efficiency and scalability of your business, while also allowing you to connect with potential investors through as many senses as possible. In Chapter 7, I talked about article drafting, email writing, and social media. Then, in Chapter 8, I discussed webinars. In this chapter, I'm going to talk about the most direct way to an investor's heart. You guessed it: It's through their stomach.

MASTERING THE ART OF THE INVESTOR DINNER

Now that you've turned your ES into a webinar that can be sent out to your investors, it's time to give the presentation in-person at an investor dinner hosted by you. As I mentioned before, some people who read the ES will only glance at the large bullet points but may listen to the entire webinar. Other investors may read the ES in detail but tune out during an online presentation. The final piece of this puzzle is meeting investors face to face, so you can give your presentation to a live audience for those who prefer a more tangible investor courtship experience.

Since you're already rock-solid on the presentation's content by this time, your focus should be on the attendee's experience, rather than the presentation itself. Your attention should be on logistics, such as the food, flow, atmosphere, level of service, sound quality, and et cetera. Excellence in these details comes with practice, trial, and error, but here are some tips to help guide you in hosting a successful investor dinner:

1. **Bring as many team members as possible.** Investors are more likely to move forward if they're comfortable with the team, and there's no better opportunity to establish connections than at an investor dinner. If there are multiple tables, you can even place your team members separate from each other so that potential investors have a greater chance of getting to know at least one of your co-workers.

2. **Encourage a few of your previous investors and/or investor-savvy friends and family members to attend and support you.** Just knowing that these key individuals are out in the

audience, likely networking with potential investors and singing your praises, will boost your confidence as a presenter. Don't get me wrong; I'm not suggesting that they blurt out, "Wow! Sounds like an amazing deal to me!" during your presentation. It just feels good to have some familiar faces in the crowd, especially ones you can rely on to create a positive crowd dynamic and overall atmosphere.

3. **Shorten the content to leave plenty of time for the Q&A.** The investor dinner is a great opportunity to go much more in-depth with the Q&A section because the event is catered towards those more likely to make an investment decision based on their personal relationship with you. When dealing with this type of potential investor, it's very important that you tailor the night to those who want to directly interact with the people they're investing with. Make sure to keep your presentation to 20-30 minutes, so you can accentuate the Q&A portion of the evening.

4. **Before the event, visualize things going wrong.** Many business coaches and self-help authors suggest visualization for reaching goals and attaining success, which is an incredibly useful tool. I've found something that's equally powerful but only rarely talked about: imagining things going wrong. Visualizing possible setbacks during your event can have a truly profound impact on your ability to overcome them when problems do arise. Then, if one or more of these instances actually happens, you've already mentally prepared to address it and can more confidently handle the situation. I was first introduced to this "fear-setting" strategy through Tim Ferris, who is a huge

advocate of it. Here are a few examples of how things can go wrong:

    a. Not enough people show up.

    b. The microphone doesn't work.

    c. The PowerPoint presentation can't be pulled up.

    d. It's too hot in the room.

5. **Don't serve dinner until the presentation is over.** Once people have the food in front of them, their focus will be on eating. The noise level will increase, which will encourage side conversations and deflect attention from the presentation. My suggestion is to provide the presentation first and pass out the food as the Q&A starts.

6. **The dinner should be nice but not extravagant.** Your audience is presumably making more than $200,000 annually, so the experience should be refined but not imply that you spend money unwisely. Depending on the event's location, I suggest spending somewhere between $50 to $80 per person, which should allow you to create the atmosphere you are seeking without going overboard.

7. **Allow invitees to RSVP with a plus-one or a plus-two, as long as they are accredited investors.** This is a good way to expand your network, make the event more enjoyable for attendees, and have a higher headcount. Please note that this plus-one suggestion would only be appropriate for 506(c) offerings, given that you would likely not have a pre-existing relationship with an invitee's additional guest(s) before the dinner.

8. **Prior to hosting the dinner, draft an email to thank guests for attending, link them to the previously recorded webinar,**

and provide a call to action. Especially with live events, it's important to have already drafted the thank-you email so that it goes out in a timely manner. I'd have it time-delayed (via MixMax) to be sent out the morning after the event. Those who attend an in-person event are the most likely to move forward, so be sure to provide them with an outline of how to do so in the thank-you email. This email should include the Executive Summary, a link to the webinar, and clear directions for what they should do if they're ready to move forward with an investment.

BE MINDFUL THAT YOUR BODY LANGUAGE COMMUNICATES YOUR INTERNAL THOUGHTS

One thing to be aware of when giving a presentation or even attending an in-person meeting is the information, and potential misinformation, your micro-movements and micro-expressions can communicate. If you project that you're uncomfortable, and your attendees don't know the root cause of your discomfort, they'll likely assume the worst. In this business, the worst means fraud.

If something is bothering you about your investor dinner, just be open about it with the attendees. For example, if you get to the restaurant at which you are presenting and the room is much warmer than you anticipated, acknowledge the issue to the attendees. This strategy is far better than simply hoping no one else notices (they will) and trying to press on with the presentation. Why? Because if you pretend the problem doesn't exist, your attendees will notice your discomfort without being able to confirm what's causing it and may assume you're uncertain about the investment or, worse, trying to swindle them.

Whatever the issue is, address it and let them know if the matter is going to be resolved or, if it can't be, apologize for the inconvenience. If it suits your personality, it helps to have a few phrases prepared for situations like this, such as, "Just so you know, I prefer to present in a sauna, so this is actually perfect."

As soon as the problem arises, be mindful that your internal thoughts, both conscious and subconscious, can communicate stress to attendees through your body language, but if you've prepared to respond to things going wrong, you can keep your micro-movements and facial expressions calm. This is one of the reasons that visualizing things going wrong is so critical. With practice, your first thought will be, "No problem. I'm ready for this." In fact, if you practice enough, you'll actually be eager to demonstrate your ability to overcome such adversity. Keeping this type of composure both improves your attendees' perspective of you as a presenter and increases their faith in your ability to overcome obstacles.

DON'T BE AFRAID TO TAKE UP PHYSICAL SPACE

Confidence is a huge component of credibility, so your physical appearance and gestures need to be on point. During your dinner event, attendees will readily experience your "stage presence" and, unfortunately, mistakes in this area can be costly, so take some time to analyze and master your physical presence.

Once you're up on stage, your muscle memory of expressing self-assurance will take over.

The most important aspect of maintaining a confident physical presence is an increased level of comfort and eagerness to take up physical space while presenting. Confident speakers stand tall, move with intention, and walk towards or physically engage with their audience. You should do the same.

On the other hand, tentative presenters look like they're sitting on an airplane trying not to touch their nearby neighbors, as if they want to be smaller and not commanding of the space. People who lack confidence in their presentation often stand stationary to the side of the room or stage, let their shoulders roll forward, and, worst of all, look down at the ground.

If you're in search of inspiration, look up "Conor McGregor Strut" on YouTube and you'll find the epitome of taking up physical space. If you aren't already familiar with Conor McGregor, he is one of the most historically significant mixed-martial artists (MMA) of all time. While his MMA record is remarkable (he holds a permanent place in history books for becoming the first Ultimate Fighting Championship fighter to hold titles in two weight classes at the same time), his fighting accolades don't scratch the surface of his impact on the entire universe of sports. In 2019, ESPN ranked him the fifth most popular athlete in the world, just two spots below LeBron James and five spots above Tiger Woods. His athletic record is impressive, but his physical presence and persona were critical to his rise in popularity. Prior to every fight, McGregor made a habit of entering the stadium with his trademark "billionaire strut," flamboyantly strutting down the aisle and swinging his arms by his side with his chest out as he walked towards the UFC octagon. Unquestionably intentional, he communicates extreme confidence both externally to the audience and internally to himself.

While I'm not suggesting that you bust through the doors of a Morton's The Steakhouse swinging your arms around with your chest stuck out to impress potential investors, I do recommend you practice a comfortable power stance and move through all of the space available to you when you speak. Having said that, if you need a little confidence boost prior to your presentation, trying out the billionaire strut in the hallway just might help.

These are the tried-and-true strategies I've learned after hosting numerous investor dinners over several years. Each suggestion will improve your ability to have a successful dinner and, thus, help you raise funds for your next closing. As long as you've warmed up your leads through your educational infrastructure, and the majority of the attendees are already interested in the types of investments you'll discuss at your dinner, your event should be a success. Worst-case scenario, you take a hit on the food and beverage costs, and everyone has a good time at your (minimal) expense.

CHAPTER 10

Communicating to Attract and Influence Investors

Befor discussing how to communicate with investors, I want to make it clear that when most people think of "selling," they think of high-pressure strategies designed to get leads across the finish line at all costs. This is because many of the most popular books on sales strategies were authored in the 1980s, prior to potential buyers being able to research the quality and reviews of specific products. Furthermore, most of these books focus exclusively on transactional sales where the buyer and the seller only interact during the exchange but aren't really tied to each other after the fact. This simply isn't the case with real estate investing today.

Remember the scene in *Glengarry Glen Ross* when Alec Baldwin delivers one of the most shining performances of his career with his unique take on a motivational sales speech? He asserts that if you can't get people to sign on the bottom line, you are useless to the firm and should get a new career in a different sector. What's his suggestion for those whose close ratios are struggling? Simple. "A-B-C.: A-Always; B-Be; C–Closing. **Always be closing.**"

When it comes to my personal real estate sales strategy, and the strategy that I suggest to anyone who is reading this book, I have a similar mnemonic device. However, the implication is basically the opposite: "A-B-D: Always-Always; B-Be; D-Disclosing. **Always be disclosing.**" If there's anything important an investor should consider prior to making the decision to invest, you should make sure they're aware of it and have seriously considered it before accepting their funds, both for legal reasons and the sake of your business.

Syndication-based real estate investments tie you to investors for many years to come, and including the wrong investor in your offering can completely blow up a deal, tarnish your reputation, and make your life extremely challenging. This is not an exaggeration. The real estate business can be very lucrative and has the potential to grant you amazing amounts of personal freedom, but if you start raising funds from investors who don't understand what they're getting into or feel pressured to move forward despite their reservations, you'll likely struggle with nightmarish investor relations issues.

In this chapter, I'll discuss several strategies for influencing and communicating to real estate–specific investors. Some of the strategies and ways I frame discussions may be counter-intuitive because it might sound like you're going to limit the number of investors who end up moving forward. To a certain extent, this is exactly what you *are* doing. To avoid the many likely head-aches that including the wrong investor can cause you, I suggest vetting your potential investors—just like they might vet you.

A NOTE ABOUT SELLING

Selling is the kind of thing people either love or hate. Having an aversion to selling stems from negative experiences we've all had with pushy salesmen, the ones who are willing to do whatever it takes to get you to purchase a product regardless of whether it will actually add value to your life. In these situations, you usually suspect the seller doesn't have your best interest at heart, so you rightfully put your guard up. Unfortunately, these same salesmen were trained to never take "no" for an answer, so your resistance only makes them feel like they're getting close to a "yes"—and they pursue you indefinitely. We've all been there, and it's terrible.

This paradigm is something that Elon Musk took so seriously, Tesla eliminated the in-person sale experience completely. He realized the potential competitive advantage he could create by controlling the entire process, ensuring clients didn't encounter the stereotypical pushy car salesmen.

Similarly, I'll attempt to instill a quality-control strategy in everyone reading this book. When it comes to real estate, if you use pushy sales tactics, it might not just create an uncomfortable feeling for the potential investor, it could result in a massive headache from a legal perspective later down the road.

Rather than cramming an investment down the throats of a potential investor, the key is to educate them, ensuring that they have a thorough understanding of the details, including the risks, and considering their investment in you and your firm a decade-long partnership (because that is exactly what it is).

BEFORE WE EVEN GET STARTED: BE AUTHENTIC

I fell in love with the syndicated model completely, as soon as I was introduced to and understood it, for all the reasons I've addressed many times in this book. There was, however, one big disincentive to starting a real estate investment company focused on the syndicated structure: Very few people knew what that term even meant.

At the time I launched Asym Capital (the company was originally named Cash Flow Connections), the term "syndication" was only frequently talked about in ultra-high net worth circles. In fact, early on in my career when I'd describe what I typically invested in, the majority of the conversation would then be spent explaining the structure itself, rather than why I found the investment compelling and how it could work for them as an investor. I viewed the public's lack of education on the topic as a major challenge to my success because there was essentially no demand for the product I was passionate about selling.

Overcoming this educational hurdle seemed like such a challenge that it was going to limit my potential investor pool and, therefore, deteriorate my bottom line. This is why when I started Asym Capital, we originally focused on helping investors invest in single-family residential properties, which were all the rage back then and didn't require as extensive an explanation.

At that time, the most popular investment vehicle was turn-key rental properties that a management company would usually buy, fix up, rent out, and sell to an investor who wanted hands-off passive cash flow. In order to ensure I was bringing something to a market where there was already considerable demand for the product, I decided to direct my marketing, branding, and educational content to that audience. Essentially, I wanted to be like everyone else. Our website looked like everyone else's; our marketing copy sounded like everyone else's; our eBook was written like everyone else's. Unsurprisingly, the results were nothing short of pathetic.

Why would I have expected anything else? What would be the reason for an investor to jump at the chance to do business with us? What was so compelling about our marketing materials when compared to anyone else's?

Perhaps we could've had marginal success, but there was one really big problem: I wasn't being authentic about the fact that I viewed commercial real estate as a far superior investment vehicle. I believed there was a ceiling on the upside potential of the single-family product type and was confident the world of syndications would produce far more favorable risk-adjusted returns. But to be honest, I was scared of overcoming that educational hurdle with the investor base. I realized the fear was really the driving factor in me attempting to convince investors to invest in something I wasn't passionate about.

I had spent roughly six months and $10,000 working on our original website and after launching, it quickly became clear that the money and time had been completely wasted. The business was intended to raise capital and help people invest in real estate, and well after launching we didn't have any investors and we didn't have any real estate. That's pretty much the most quintessential example of a business failure I can think of.

After quite a bit of soul searching, I realized it was time to pivot and focus exclusively on commercial real estate that helped investors invest through syndications. After all, this was the vehicle I truly believed in, and I knew I could transfer that passion to potential investors if given the opportunity.

This is when I really started building the infrastructure outlined in this book, which eventually allowed us to experience the success we've earned over the years. As soon as the infrastructure was created and the steps outlined in this book were completed, the money started coming in. There's literally no telling where I'd be had I never made that pivot.

The key takeaway here is that you have to be authentic in your messaging. When you are trying to influence someone, especially when it comes to money, most of their attention is on trying to answer one question: Is this person trying to take advantage of me? If you are being inauthentic, they'll pick up on that, and they'll always assume the worst. In fact, you might never know this is why people are passing on your available investment offering, because they won't tell you.

I can't emphasize enough that whenever you have a meeting, lunch, or coffee, or are writing articles, telling stories, and authoring a book, be absolutely as authentic and honest as you can be. If you ever feel like you are pushing an investor to invest in something you have reservations about, stop immediately and contemplate if you are being true to yourself and your values.

Being inauthentic will result in painfully low close ratios, low dollars invested, and a lack of success. More importantly, it will get you in the bad habit of trying to sell something that you aren't passionate about, which can lead you down a rocky road in this business. Being transparent and honest will have the opposite effect and help you scale much more quickly.

SYSTEMATIZING YOUR SCHEDULING PROCESS

Now that I've addressed some common reservations about selling, as well as the discussion about being authentic, it's time to dive in and close some deals. The first step in this process is to create a systematic sales funnel that's efficient and scalable. Your ever-growing infrastructure of educational content is certainly going to help, but at the end of the day, you'll likely need to communicate directly to potential investors before they'll move forward. This is the last stage of the investment process, and if you don't focus some efforts on ensuring this part runs smoothly, you'll impede your chances of succeeding after all the hard work you put in on the front end.

While some people are huge proponents of in-person meetings, I usually avoid them due to the inefficiency associated with driving around in traffic, as well as the increased likelihood of the meeting attendees being late or missing the meeting altogether. I understand all of the benefits of in-person meetings, but I just find that being in my office on the phone is most efficient and effective for me.

I always do my best to accommodate if an investor is adamant on meeting in person, but only after we have at least one phone call to ensure that we're on the same page. If you're like me and prefer phone calls, start implementing a policy that requires a phone call prior to an in-person meeting. You'll be surprised how much time you'll save.

If you're going to be focusing on phone calls, you should have an efficient system for setting up the meeting and conducting the call. Thankfully, scheduling tools that help automate the process have seen an upswing in popularity, so you don't have to waste time trying to find out when both you and your potential investors are free. Even if this saves you three minutes per scheduled meeting, you'll likely save hours upon hours each year.

Setting Up the Call

One of my favorite efficiency tools is an automated scheduling system called ScheduleOnce (www.scheduleonce.com). This app connects to your online calendar, and when you share your personalized link to a potential client, they're able to see all of your availability and select a time block that works for them. This way, you can avoid the back-and-forth of trying to schedule a call.

Because this technology is so advantageous, more and more people are getting used to it. However, when I email someone my link, I still like to give them the opportunity to provide me with some of their preferred times, rather than use my automated system. Here's what my typical outgoing email looks like, if it's clear we need to schedule a call:

Hey [insert first name],

Great question. Would you be interested in setting up a call for us to discuss in more detail? I'm happy to correspond via email if that's your preference, but I always prefer to jump on a call so you can have the opportunity to ask follow-up questions. If that works on your end, please let me know some of your free times this week for a 30-minute call. Alternatively, you can follow this link to see my free times and select a 30-minute block that is convenient for your schedule.

[insert link to scheduling app]

Thanks.

I use this language so frequently I even created an email text template in MixMax that I can insert into any email by pressing a keyboard shortcut. I've used a combination of this MixMax template and the scheduling link thousands of times. These simple tools have likely saved me more than a hundred hours over the years. ScheduleOnce has a free version, so the risk is exceptionally limited; Calendly (www.calendly.com) is a comparable competitor. I highly suggest implementing a tool like this to streamline the scheduling process.

Why Are You Scheduling a Call?

I'm sure you're excited to get started using these tools, but prior to sending out a single request for a phone call, it's important to identify and characterize why you are setting up the call in the first place. From my perspective, there are usually two main types of calls to conduct with potential investors during the sales process:

1. Introductory calls
2. Due diligence calls

I really like to keep these two types of calls separate, as I prefer to schedule at least 30 minutes with new investors to introduce myself and learn more about them. If they're interested in continuing the conversation and discussing the details of a particular offering during the initial call, I usually answer any questions they have after we get acquainted, but then set up a follow-up call to specifically focus on due diligence items. This will help the flow of things, so that neither you nor the potential investor feel like you're rushing into the details without first establishing a genuine connection.

INTRODUCTORY CALLS

The main goal of introductory calls is to establish rapport with potential investors who, of course, are more likely to move forward with operators they know, like, and trust. This is why it's critical to establish a bond prior to getting into the nitty-gritty of a particular deal. Once you jump into the details of an investment opportunity, the investor will focus on analytics, such as the return profile, rather than the people they're making a bet on. If you get in the habit of immediately jumping into the details of an offering before you've had the opportunity to develop a fundamental relationship, you'll find it next to impossible to truly stand out amongst your competitors and even extremely interested investors will routinely end up passing on the opportunity at the last minute.

With so many real estate deals in the market and very little difference between each company's respective offering decks, investors need to have a thorough understanding of who you are as a person, or they're unlikely to move forward. This is the case regardless of how analytical they sound over the phone, their level of experience in real estate, or their professional background.

In order for an investor to trust you with their hard-earned capital, they need to know what motivates you, what your moral compass is like, and how you've overcome challenging situations in the past. Essentially, they need personal context in order for the claims you make to have any substance. This is one of the reasons we prefer that each new investor sets up an introductory call with us in order to get to know each other before they invest in one of our offerings.

Taking Control of the Call and Setting Its Agenda

The first moments of an introductory call are the most important because it's at this time that a potential investor will jump to a conclusion about whether or not you are competent and should be trusted with their capital. It's critical that you quickly take control of the call by announcing its structure and agenda within the first 30 seconds of the potential investor answering the phone. This will show the investor that you know what you're doing, have done it before many times, and have created a system to streamline this process.

One of my favorite books of all time is *Pitch Anything* by Oren Klaff. If you haven't already read it, add it to your list immediately. The book is revolutionary in its analysis of why people make decisions, and the science-backed theories are balanced out with quality storytelling about high-pressure, multi-million-dollar pitches. There are two critical concepts discussed in the book that I want to be sure you implement immediately to help improve your entire sales process, Time Framing and Prizing.

Time Framing is a strategy for establishing credibility by confirming that your time is scarce. In this instance, you'll accomplish this by stating the start and end time of the call, as well as outlining the call's agenda upfront. I've made sure this book is jam-packed with tips that make reading it time well spent, but this simple strategy is, without a doubt, one of the most important takeaways in this book.

Here's what Time Framing should sound like:

Hey [insert first name], this is [insert your full name] with [insert your company name]. Is now a good time for you? Great. Just to let you know, I have us blocked for 30 minutes and I have another investor call that starts right at [insert current time plus 30 minutes]. So, if it's ok with you, let's jump right into it.

This short little paragraph should guarantee your call starts off on the right foot, most importantly by putting potential investors at ease because they know they won't be sucked into an endless pitch that will drone on forever. Additionally, it establishes that your time is valuable and other potential investors are interested in your offerings.

Once you've confirmed that the meeting time still works and have outlined the duration of the call, outline the call's schedule so both you and the potential investor are on the same page. Here's what this should sound like:

First, I'd love to hear more about your background and your experience in the real estate sector. Then, I'd like to share a bit about my background and our investing strategy as a company, and where we see the opportunity currently in the marketplace. Afterwards, I'd be happy to answer any questions you have. Sound good?

Doing this makes it clear that you've been through this process many times, as well as establishes that you're the one dictating the pace. This will put a lot of investors at ease because they'll become aware that they're dealing with a savvy, time-conscious professional.

Remember This: You Are the Prize

The other concept from *Pitch Anything* is Prizing. This is absolutely critical to implement during introductory calls, especially when you're just getting started. One of the quickest ways to sabotage getting your deal funded is to project neediness or desperation, the worst deal killers that exist in the world of capital raising. Regardless of how much you know about the investment, how high the returns are, or how robust your firm's background is, if an investor senses neediness, their interest in the deal will evaporate.

Fortunately, there's a way to avoid this: Ensure that both you and your potential investor know that you and your offering are the prize, not their money.

If you're new to the game, it may be challenging to convince yourself that you don't need a potential investor's money because every single $25,000 investment seems like it's life or death. But don't worry if this sounds like you; in time, you'll build the confidence that the money is going to come your way regardless. While faking it until you make is certainly more advantageous than begging for investors to fund your deal, actually arriving at the realization that there's plenty of money out there will allow you to eradicate the neediness factor without being inauthentic about your own thoughts.

The reality is that investment capital is one of the most objectively available commodities in the world. Want proof? There are literally trillions of dollars being invested into bonds with a negative interest rate. That's right. Millions of people all over the globe are investing in ventures that, if they perform exactly as projected, will lose money. Not only are these investments being made constantly, they're some of the most common investment vehicles in all of the global financial markets.

If you're reading this book, you probably have access to some of the most desirable investment vehicles on planet Earth. You're also likely already well on your way to surrounding yourself with some of the ultra-high performers in the real estate market. If you're someone who's fully enveloped by the world of alternative investments, you may start to incorrectly get the sense that "everyone" has access to similarly desirable opportunities. The sheer size of the negative interest rate bond market alone proves that nothing could be further from the truth.

The types of offerings we've dedicated all of this time to are still far outside the realm of what most people are aware of and have access to. Most likely, real estate isn't playing nearly as significant a role in your potential investors' portfolios as it should be. Keep all of this in mind when communicating with investors, and it will certainly help you drop the neediness.

Time Framing and Prizing are both outlined in more detail in E48 of the *Cash Flow Connections Real Estate Podcast*, "How to Get Investor's Attention, Keep It, and Pitch Anything," with Oren Klaff himself.

TIPS FOR THE INTRODUCTORY CALL

If you use the two strategies outlined above, you'll establish enough credibility up front to ensure that you start the call on the right foot. This will allow you the opportunity to really focus on the key goals of the introductory call.

Here are a few items I suggest:

1. **Establish their status as an accredited investor.** This is obviously critical if you are raising capital for a 506(c) offering.

2. **Learn about their background and their investing experience.** Take note of what they say, as it'll paint a clear picture of how sophisticated of an investor they are and, therefore, how you'll communicate with them when it's time for you to speak.

3. **Learn about their motivations to invest.** Listen carefully here. Don't check out during these calls because "you've heard it all before." Everything a potential investor says is a clue to their perspective and motivating factors for having the call in the first place. Once you have a good grasp of what has motivated them to consider investing in non-traditional investments like the ones you offer, you can then focus your responses to directly address those motivations. Listen for key indicators, such as they're fearful of the stock market; they recently sold a property and are looking to roll over funds into new asset classes; they want diversification out of a particular sector of real estate and would like to invest into another asset class; or they want to take a more passive approach to investing. Listening to these little nuances will allow you to learn about your potential inventor, build that relationship, and know what to focus on when the time comes to explain the benefits of your particular investment. As they're speaking, you should make mental notes of what you can infer from their responses. Are they type of investor motivated by the fear of missing out on an opportunity, or are they more motivated by the benefits? Do they need immediate cash flow to pay off expenses, or do they plan on using the gains from their investments for retirement later on? Picking up on these

details will help you optimize the conversation and allow you to speak in a language tailored to be most impactful for the particular investor.

4. **Share your "last-straw moment."** Describe the point in your investing career when you realized that traditional investments weren't going to get you where you wanted to be financially. For a lot of people, 2008 was a major wake-up call. Another common last-straw moment for real estate entrepreneurs is related to dealing with an illness, either their own or someone in their family. This section of the call is about being honest and authentic, so identify when you realized that real estate was an excellent way to achieve your financial goals and share it with your potential investor. Make sure you go into detail and are relatable. This personal anecdote will provide a potential investor with a deeper look into your background and ethos.

5. **Share your "key motivating factor."** In order to establish rapport, it's important for you to share your internal motivation to help other people invest. This is what gets you out of bed every morning. My personal main motivation is that I feel morally obligated to help people get money out of the stock market due to its unpredictability. When I share this with people, they can tell that I'm interested in their success as an investor and am aligned with their pursuit of diversification.

6. **As you are telling your own story, directly address their motivations for investing, affirm the challenges with other investments, and discuss how the benefits of your particular investment strategy apply to their investment goals.**

During this stage of the call, make sure to restate the topics they brought up in your own words and confirm that they can significantly mitigate those challenges by considering an investment in your offering.

7. **Share your general investment thesis.** Before getting deep into due diligence, it's important to provide investors with a high-level overview of why you are interested in your particular niche. This provides context for the entire business, as opposed to just a one-off investment. For Asym, our investment thesis is centered around recession-resistant assets. We outline our investment thesis as follows:

In short, all types of real estate do well when the economy is booming, and the lending market is loose. The key is to identify real estate that performs well in all stages of the cycle because then you are getting the best of both worlds. Essentially, we're looking for product types in which there is an inverse correlation between the overall economy and the demand for the product.

Iron out your own investment thesis and be sure to connect it to your personal motivations to invest. This will tie the entire conversation together and create a clear pathway to a due diligence call.

After you've learned some key details about your potential investor, shared a bit about yourself, and confirmed that their motivations to invest are valid, a few specific questions about your available offering will inevitably arise. Even though the call wasn't intended for due diligence, it's ok to answer these questions, as long as you've accomplished the previously stated goals of the introductory call.

However, do not, under any circumstances, go over the 30-minute time period on the first call. It's absolutely critical in the beginning of the relationship with a new investor to establish that your time is valuable and scarce. Even if it means ending the call before all of their questions have been answered, insist that you need to run to your next call, meeting, or work-related activity.

Here's how you could wrap things up:

Thanks again for your time today. I'm glad we connected. As far as next steps, I'll email you the Executive Summary for our current offering, as well as our webinar we recently conducted on the topic. Expect those in just a moment. I'll also send my scheduling link so that you can set up another call if you have further questions. Sound good?

Sounds good.

Perfect. If I don't hear from you in five days, is it ok if I reach out, just to get a good sense of your interest?

Yes, that's no problem at all.

It's also a nice touch to have a reason to send them some of your educational content after you get off the call. For example, if they asked you why you prefer multi-family investments over single-family investments, and you've already written an article on this topic, don't miss the opportunity to share this resource with them. This puts those long hours you spent creating the content to use, and sharing the resources you created will also boost your credibility.

POST-INTRODUCTORY CALL FOLLOW UP

If I don't hear from an investor for about five days after sending them the post-call materials, whether or not they were explicitly interested in moving forward, I usually send a follow-up email that's something similar to this:

Hey [insert first name],

I hope you're doing well. I wanted to follow up and see if you had any further questions about our current offering. If so, please follow this link [insert link to scheduler] to schedule a 30-minute or one-hour block that's convenient for you. Of course, if you would rather correspond via email, that's no problem.

As a reminder, the commitment deadline for this offering is [insert date], and we anticipate it'll be oversubscribed prior to that date.

Thank you.

From my experience, if you don't receive a response from this email, one additional personalized follow-up email is appropriate.

Anything more than that may create a sense of desperation or feel like you're flooding their inbox. If they're interested in the offer, they'll schedule an additional call or send further questions via email.

If you don't hear back at that point, I suggest waiting until you have an upcoming investor dinner in their area, are conducting a new webinar, or when something else noteworthy takes place (such as a sale of a previously owned asset) before directly contacting them again. Any of the aforementioned scenarios will give you enough justification to get in touch with them about your offering and re-open the discussion without it seeming unwarranted.

DUE DILIGENCE CALLS

The focus of the introductory call is to get to know one another and provide an insight into the big-picture thesis of your business. It's only supposed to be a snapshot, so it's very likely that some people will schedule a follow-up call to discuss the specifics of your current offering and your business. We'll refer to this communication as due diligence calls. These calls are up to one hour and allow the investors to unearth details about the particular investment.

Once you get to the point in the sales process where a potential investor has requested a follow-up call, there's a very good chance that they're interested in moving forward. The goal here is simply to educate the investor, answer questions, clarify how much work you've put in, and explain your expertise.

Here are a few tips for your due diligence calls:

1. **Prior to the call, practice answering challenging questions with a friend or business partner.** Simply being an expert isn't enough. You must be able to communicate your knowledge effectively and confidently, which will only come with practice. Write down as many questions as you can possibly come up with and have your friend ask them at random, as well as any follow-up questions that come to mind. Request that they ask you to clarify anything that doesn't immediately make sense.

2. **Outline the key assumptions of your offering and confirm that they're conservative in nature by providing historical data points, comps, or other measures.** Statements about your key assumptions should sound like this:

    a. *Historically, we've raised rents by about 4.8% per year while we bring the property up to market rates, but we only assumed 4% per year in the projections to keep the assumptions conservative and achievable.*

    b. *The city planning commission has informed us they just agreed to the zoning plans of a 110-property housing development only two miles from the property. We're confident the additional traffic of this development will bring attention to the property, but we didn't factor that into our assumptions.*

3. **Discuss a few conservative assumptions that weren't outlined in the Executive Summary.** In every deal, I like to keep a few additional ways that I've been conservative in my back pocket for due diligence calls, if it's appropriate to

do so. For example, let's say I have a self-storage property I'm raising capital for. In an effort to remain conservative, I might drastically reduce, or even eliminate, the forecasted income from merchandise sales in the pro forma, which will amount to a few hundred dollars per month. Then, when I'm on a due diligence call, if an investor starts to ask about our assumptions in order to gauge how conservative or aggressive we're being, I'll reveal that this additional padding in the numbers exists and explain why we are well-positioned to outperform on that line item. Sophisticated investors who uncover the ways that you've worked to make the numbers more conservative will view this very favorably, especially since you're doing it behind closed doors.

4. **During the conversation, confirm that the potential investor understands the investment's time horizon to avoid future confusion.** Dealing with an investor who "absolutely needs to get their money out" can be a real headache in the world of syndications. Not only should they know how long the time horizon of the investment is, but they should be very confident that they won't need their invested capital until after the investment has been taken full cycle. Being clear about this shows investors that you're looking out for all parties involved, as opposed to pushing every investor to fund as soon as possible.

5. **If you don't know the answer to a question, just be honest, find out the answer, and get back to them as quickly as possible.** Not knowing the answer to a challenging question isn't a deal killer, but what can kill the deal is not

following up to provide them with the answer. Use your CRM software or set an email reminder to ensure they receive the information, then ingrain that answer in your memory for the next time the topic comes up.

6. **Remind them of the investment deadline, as well as the fact that the opportunity will likely be oversubscribed prior to the deadline.** Remember, real estate investors are successful and busy people. You have to establish that the investment is time sensitive and scarce, or they won't make it a priority.

7. **Ask them if they're interested in investing.** Don't make the mistake of going through all this hard work just to let the phone call end without asking if they'd like to invest. Many times, if you make it this far, they'll be ready to move forward. However, it's very important that you actually ask them, rather than rely on them to come out and commit to invest.

Due diligence conversations often get down to the nitty gritty, so you have to be prepared to refine your own due diligence process and overall understanding of the investment. I've had many Ivy League and business school graduates schedule call after call to get into the minutia, but it truly doesn't bother me—and it shouldn't bother you either. Here's why: The deeper they go, the more likely they're going to realize how favorable your offerings are.

Don't be discouraged, don't give up, and take something away from every call. Someone is taking your offering seriously, enough to free up time in their busy schedule to learn more about what you've been working so hard on. Be grateful. Additionally, if they go deep into due diligence and end up moving forward, it's a great vote of confidence in your thesis, thought process, and the validity of the investment.

CHAPTER 11

Answering Frequently
Asked Questions

As you can tell from everything I've focused on so far, my system for closing investor capital is really a knowledge-based close strategy. My goal is to ensure that every investor knows as much about the opportunity as necessary for them to make an educated decision on whether or not it's a good fit. In order to put them in this position, you'll need to have a thorough understanding of many aspects of the investment you're raising capital for.

As you go through these due diligence calls, you'll find that many of the same questions will be asked over and over again. In this section, I'll discuss some of the most common questions, along with my corresponding thoughts. My hope is that sharing my perspective will deepen your understanding of each topic so that you can put the answer into your own words, which is always more useful than simply providing a scripted response.

Why should I passively invest as opposed to just buying a property myself?

You may encounter potential investors who aren't familiar with the passive approach to investing or have already had success in real estate as sole owner/operator. From their perspective, why should they relinquish control to the operating partner when they can probably handle it all themselves? This is common, especially when dealing with accredited investors, so don't be discouraged. Once they've been exposed to the world of passive investing, they'll eventually see the enormous benefits of the strategy. In fact, many talented active real estate owners have made significant passive investments in an effort to further diversify their portfolio.

Here are a few things I like to discuss regarding this topic:

1. **When someone is investing in highly complicated asset classes such as commercial real estate, a top-tier operator can bring great value to the opportunity—enough that they should make up for the fact that they're receiving some of the proceeds of the offering.** The more complicated the investment vehicle, the more value an operating partner can bring to the table. In a relatively simple asset class like single-family residences, there isn't a substantial difference between best-in-class owners and mom-and-pop owners. Therefore, an operator isn't as valuable. However, in a 200+ unit multi-family apartment, which functions more

like an operating business, an operator could provide invaluable systems, processes, relationships, and know-how, justifying their participation in the offering. Because of this, the return profile might actually be similar to what an active investor may achieve on their own, but the passive approach doesn't require the investor's time once the investment has been made. To me, this is the strongest case to be made for passive investing.

2. **The passive approach allows investors to experience diversification across multiple geographies, tenant types, product types, management styles, operators, and many more aspects of the real estate sector.** One can't be an expert in everything. Diversification, however, is critical when building a portfolio. From my perspective, the only way to achieve this goal is to have a portion of their portfolio invested in passive investments that are managed by leading operators in a particular asset class. As a tie-in to #1 above: Even if the potential investor has had success owning and operating real estate in more complicated asset classes, it's very likely that they're either over-allocated to that particular asset class or don't have a significant market advantage in the asset class because they aren't exclusively focused on it.

3. **Due to the distinction between the class of shares between the General Partner (operating partner/sponsor) and the Limited Partner (passive investor), the sponsor is the only party to incur credit and liability risk.** This is a *major* value-add for passive investors because it grants them access to low-cost debt financing through the sponsor's track record

without incurring the risk associated with personally guaranteeing a loan. Eliminating these challenges of investing in real estate categorically shifts the total risk profile of the investment without ever significantly deteriorating the returns.

4. **Investing in passive syndications allows investors to rely on highly sophisticated operators who stand to gain millions of dollars if they're able to deliver to their investors.** This is in stark contrast to typical active investments, where the property values are limited because the investment capital is generally all coming from one person. High-value commercial properties with the potential of producing millions of dollars' worth of gains not only attracts high-caliber people, but also genuinely aligns the interest of the operating partner and the investor. Unfortunately, this often isn't the case in single-family houses, where investors may worry about fraudulent property managers who skew invoices in hopes of skimming a few hundred dollars.

I find the points outlined above extremely compelling and have built my entire investment approach around them. If you're interested in hearing me make a further case for passive investing, check out a debate I had on the topic at www.raisingcapitalfor-realestate.com.

At the end of the day, despite how persuasive the points outlined above are, sometimes investors may be intrigued by the world of passive syndications but are reluctant to give up control. If they seem like the kind of investor that's going to continuously struggle with that, a passive LP investment probably won't be a good fit. If control is their driving factor, just be honest with them—suggest that they stick to active investments. Of course, let them know you'll keep them on your list so that if their preference changes, they'll have access to future offerings.

Why don't I have many voting rights?

As I discussed previously, most passive syndicated investments don't allow investors to maintain many voting rights. Accordingly, the overwhelming majority of a passive investor's due diligence process will be focused on the operating partner, and they'll have very little insight into the other passive investors in the offering. Ultimately, passive investors are relying on the operating partner's expertise. If the passive investors in a deal retain significant voting rights, they're allowing their investment capital to be controlled by other passive investors whom they know very little about and who are likely not experts when it comes to this particular investment.

Here's an extreme example: Let's say there is an offering where the operator is raising a total of $2,000,000. In this scenario, let's assume that one passive investor invests $50,000 and another investor invests the remaining $1,950,000. If the operating agreement grants the passive investors a significant amount of control via voting rights, and their vote is based on their proportional investment amount, the $50,000 investor's entire investment is subject to the whims of another passive investor whom they likely know nothing about.

Furthermore, the general public tends to make the wrong decisions during stressful times. For example, if the market starts to slide, you don't want the other passive investors forcing the operating partner to sell. This is just one reason why it's usually best to defer to the operating partner to make tough choices.

I know this may seem counterintuitive, but many times it's best to limit the voting rights of passive investors to action items like the removal of the manager or raising additional capital for an unexpected improvement to the property.

What happens if I need the money during the hold period?

Despite all of the warnings that you put in your Executive Summary, webinar, and live presentation, investors might still have an unfortunate misunderstanding about their ability to buy and sell their interest as they please. It's critical for investors to understand on the front end that investments in syndications should always be considered illiquid and non-transferrable, meaning that any dollars invested shouldn't be needed during the duration of the hold period. Just be upfront about this, and it'll alleviate future headaches.

However, it's also important that you have a mechanism in place to help an investor if they have an emergency requiring that they sell their interest. Think about it. Even if financial emergencies only happen 1% of the time, if you plan on having hundreds of investors, you'll likely have a few issues throughout your career.

Typically, when an investor needs to sell their shares in a real estate syndication, the most critical component is time, so keep this in mind when you draft your legal documents.

One legal provision we include in our operating agreement is that we grant the General Partner (GP) of the offering a Right of First Refusal to purchase the shares of any investor who wishes to sell their interest without notifying all of the other investors. This way, the problem can be solved while also limiting the amount of time it takes to complete the transfer.

If you have a similar clause, it's important to reiterate to the potential investor that this provision doesn't set the expectation that the GP *will* purchase the shares; it's just the first line of defense for resolving the situation. In our offering documents, if the GP decides not to purchase the shares, the next step is to sell the shares to another investor who's already in the offering, which decreases the amount of administrative duties related to completing the transfer.

We also clarify upfront that there will be a $1,000+ fee for anyone who sells their shares before the investment comes full term. From an administrative standpoint, effectuating one of these transfers is fairly burdensome and requires amending legal documents and other administrative duties that shouldn't (and won't) be paid for by other investors in the offering.

Establish a system for resolving these sorts of issues, then be as transparent as possible to potential investors, and when the issue comes up, as it undoubtedly will, handle the problem as quickly as possible.

What are the tax implications of this investment?

Any time you get a question about the tax or legal implications of an investment, it's always best to start and end with a disclaimer that you're not a CPA or an attorney. Also, always advise the interested investor to consult with their financial and legal professionals prior to making a decision about investing.

When I first entered the real estate business, I always thought people who frequently made this disclaimer were being a bit over-cautious. As I learned more about the implications of answering these sorts of questions, I began to understand why it's not only just industry standard, but it's prudent to do so. Even if you are a financial or legal professional, you still need to make the disclaimer that they need to seek *their own* counsel on any legal and tax matters.

If and when I'm asked questions about tax implications, after providing them with a brief disclaimer, I usually outline some of the favorable tax incentives for investing in real estate. Most notably, I mention the benefit of depreciation, which is an income tax deduction. In short, while real estate values generally appreciate, the physical components of the property generally lose value during the hold as a result of wear and tear. The appliances, roof, and electrical all "depreciate" and will eventually need to be replaced. The Internal Revenue Service (IRS) understands and accounts for this by offering an income deduction for owning depreciating assets.

Here's how it works: Let's say you buy a commercial property for $10,000,000. The tax assessor's estimate of the land value is $3,000,000, and the building value estimate is $7,000,000. The land value won't count towards the depreciation calculation, but the building value will be depreciated over 39 years. This would imply that each year, there would be a $179,487 "loss" for tax purposes ($7,000,000/39 = $179,487). (Please note that this calculation doesn't include any benefits of a cost segregation study, which can sometimes increase the annual write-off property owners can receive.) You can learn more about depreciation by listening to the *Cash Flow Connections Real Estate Podcast*, E133: "How You Can Save Money Through Cost Segregation."

Just remember that depreciation is a "phantom" expense. Investors aren't actually writing a check for the "loss" that they're experiencing.

When someone invests in one of our offerings, they invest in an LLC that holds, directly or through another entity, interest in a property or properties. Essentially, we pass the benefits of owning the property, including depreciation, through the LLC to the investor.

In most real estate deals, depreciation and other tax write-offs allow all cash flow during the hold period to be received tax-deferred. This means that regardless of the amount of dollars received from cash flow during the hold period, the annual taxable gain will usually be net negative, or very close to it. Of course, if the property is later sold at a gain, there will be a tax based on long-term capital gains rates, as well as a tax for **depreciation recapture** for any gains of sales made from the depreciated asset. For more information about deprecation recapture, please review this article: https://www.investopedia.com/terms/d/depreciationrecapture.asp.

Sometimes, investors have the misconception that if they invest in a multiple property fund, they won't get the tax benefits of owning property. This is not necessarily the case. *Most* private real estate funds are structured in such a way that investors receive the benefits of depreciation, but from multiple properties instead of just one. Technically speaking, this can vary for a variety of reasons, so make sure you understand the tax implications of your specific investment.

At the end of each tax year, investors will receive a K-1, which is a tax document for investments in partnerships. The K-1 shows the investor their annual loss or gain and will be presented to their CPA to file their taxes accurately.

When it comes to explaining the tax situation of a typical syndicated real estate investment, this is a really good starting point. As mentioned above, always remember to suggest that an investor consults with their CPA and attorney before making the decision to invest.

What happens if I invest through a self-directed retirement account (SDIRA)?

Since the 1970s, U.S. citizens have had the ability to "self-direct" their retirement accounts. This allows the account owner full control over the account and gives them freedom to invest in a diverse group of alternative asset classes, such as real estate, in order to pay for their retirement without being forced into stocks and bonds. Unfortunately, due to pervasive marketing campaigns conducted by large retirement account companies, only a very small percentage of people know they can invest in these alternative investments while saving for their retirement.

The legal requirements surrounding self-directed retirement are incredibly complex and strict, thus every SDIRA is required to be overseen by a custodian that's subject to government audits. My preferred SDIRA custodian firm is uDirect IRA Services (www.udirectira.com).

Generally speaking, having an SDIRA is extremely favorable for investors because the vehicle allows for tax-advantaged real estate investments, therefore drastically increasing the rate at which the account can grow in size.

However, there are a few caveats to investing in most real estate deals within an SDIRA, the most important of which is the Unrelated Business Income Tax (UBIT), more specifically, the Unrelated Debt Financed Income (UDFI) tax. (Since it's common for investors to refer to the UDFI tax as "UBIT" in these discussions, I'll do so here as well.)

Regardless of the tax-advantaged status of the SDIRA, there's a tax on the percentage of the opportunity's gains that are attributed to debt financing. Real estate is typically purchased with debt, so it's common that UBIT will play a role in most SDIRA investments.

For example, if your SDIRA invests in a property that's acquired via 70% debt financing, 70% of the gains will be taxed, regardless of the tax-advantaged status of the SDIRA. However, this might sound much worse than it actually is. Remember our conversation about depreciation?

Typically, the depreciation expense discussed earlier in this book is not allowed when investing through SDIRAs, but depreciation and other operating expense deductions are allowed to be received when using debt financing on a purchase. This is a way of counterbalancing the issues related to UBIT.

Usually, this results in no taxable "income" during the hold period, with UBIT being due only when the property is sold, and the gains are realized. Even then, an SDIRA is only required to file a tax return and pay UBIT if there's more than $1,000 of Unrelated Business Taxable Income (UBTI) earned by the SDIRA across all of its investments, as the SDIRA is allowed a $1,000 specific deduction. The SDIRA's UBTI is taxed at trust income tax rates, which are the following for 2019 at the federal level:

Unrelated Business Taxable Income	Up To	Tax Rate
$0	$2,600	10%
>$2,600	$9,300	24%
>$9,300	$12,750	35%
>$12,750	$Infinite	37%

Let's say you invested $50,000 via your SDIRA and received $50,000 of taxable gains (net of depreciation and expense deductions). If you used debt financing to finance 70% of your purchase, then 70% of the gains (above the $1,000 deduction) would be subject to UBIT.

$50,000 * 70% = $35,000 (gains attributed to debt financing) - $1,000 (the $1,000 deduction) = $34,000 of income to taxed at the trust income tax rates above

If UBTI Is Between	Tax Rate	The Tax Due Is:
$0-$2,600	10%	$260
>$2,600 - $9,300 = $6,700	24%	$1,608
> $9,300 - $12,750 = $3,450	35%	$1,207.50
> $12,750 - $34,000 = $21,250	37%	$7,012.50
		$10,088 = Total

This would result in you receiving $39,912 in gains from the sale net of UBIT, instead of the original $50,000 amount before UBIT was factored in.

You can use this math on a financial calculator to accurately estimate how your specific investment will perform, but let's say you incur this $50,000 gain and subsequent $10,088 tax over a 10-year period; you're likely talking about a difference of going from a 12% Internal Rate of Return (IRR) pre-UBIT to an 11% IRR after UBIT or something similarly negligible. If you're interested in seeing how big of an impact UBIT will make on your investment, input your specific cash flow assumptions into Excel and run your own IRR calculations, but my guess is that it will be near the 1-2% IRR range.

Please note, these are all hypothetical examples and a general overview of this topic. They are not to be construed as tax advice at all. I recommend you consult with a CPA before making any investment decisions.

Looking at this from a net-net perspective, it's still possible to achieve highly favorable risk-adjusted returns even after UBIT is accounted for. In fact, my personal SDIRA is invested in investments that are structured just like the example above because the net result is still extremely compelling.

In short, UBIT will impact most real estate investments made through SDIRAs because the majority use debt financing. However, this shouldn't deter people from considering investing in syndicated leveraged real estate investments within their SDIRA.

There's no need to dive right into all of these details if an investor asks about self-directed retirement, but I wanted to provide you with as much context as possible so that you'll be able to address any follow-up questions they may ask on the topic.

What are the major risks of the offering?

This is the most common question you'll receive from potential investors. Prepare to answer this question truthfully and discuss the ways in which you've worked to mitigate any potential risks.

With any passive investment, the biggest risks are challenges associated with the operator and the onsite manager. I'm transparent about this reality from the start, then I discuss some of the steps we've taken to greatly reduce the likelihood that we'll have challenges in these areas.

Here are a few steps we take when conducting due diligence on an operating partner, as well as the key companies that'll be involved in the management of the asset:

1. Implement a systematized due diligence process and checklist
2. Run background checks on their key team members
3. Conduct onsite visits
4. Interview professional references, including insurers, contractors, accountants, and legal counsel
5. Conduct a review of the property manager's systems, processes, and software

This is a good time to share how you've explored every detail of the offering in order to feel comfortable with the opportunity and the team members involved. Your processes are likely far above and beyond what potential investors have the time, capacity, and expertise to do, so you'll likely validate your role in this opportunity by providing this information.

Something else that can also ease any investor's uncertainty is to hear that other savvy investors decided to move forward with you. Mention anyone that's invested in your opportunity who has an extensive background in real estate or finance, or who went to business school. I'd also include a high-level overview of some of the due diligence questions those sophisticated investors asked prior to moving forward. You don't need to replay the conversation word for word, but making it clear that other savvy investors moved forward with the investment will really boost your credibility.

How are you aligned with your investors' incentives?

One of the many benefits of investing in real estate, as opposed to exclusively investing in stocks, is that investors in real estate get the benefit of being highly financially aligned with the people they're investing in. It's important to highlight exactly how you've worked to align your incentives for long-term performance, as opposed to just working to get a deal funded. Here are the best items to focus on when it comes to explaining how your incentives align with your investors' :

1. **Describe the percentage of your proceeds that are based on performance above a preferred return, as opposed to upfront fees.** Let's say you're likely to receive a 2% upfront fee for pre-close duties and an additional 1% of capital raised on average based on performance, only once the preferred

return has been paid and investors have received their capital back. Using this example, if the investment was a 10-year hold, that would mean you'd stand to receive 2% from upfront fees plus 10% (1% annually for 10 years = 10%) from performance above the preferred return, which would equate to 12% of capital raised as your total compensation. In this situation, roughly 83% (10%/12%) of your compensation is derived from performance.

2. **If you (or someone in the GP) are putting up your personal balance sheet as collateral for a loan, make sure investors are aware of that.** Typically, if a bank is going to grant someone a loan for millions of dollars, they usually require that the loan guarantor provides proof that they have more than enough funds to pay the loan back if something goes wrong. It's true that most commercial loans are non-recourse, meaning that if the borrower defaults, the bank seizes the property, but can't pursue the borrower personally. However, there are many cases where banks have circumvented those clauses and pursued the loan guarantor, especially if they believe the GP acted in bad faith. While the potential for making millions of dollars is certainly a motivating factor for a lot of real estate investors, doing whatever it takes to ensure that they don't lose millions of dollars can be equally as motivating. Make sure investors understand that you and your partners are motivated by both the carrot and the stick: You have the upside of the proceeds above the preferred return and the downside that's associated with guaranteeing the loan.

3. **If you, your friends, and your family members are investing, communicate that to potential investors.** When an investor asks about incentive alignment, they're really trying to figure out how strongly you believe in the investment offering and whether or not you'll stick around if things start to get challenging. There's no better way to make your intentions clear than if you, your family, and your friends have invested. Granted, you could be dead wrong, but if you've helped the people you love the most invest in the offering, it's clear you believe in its downside protection and upside potential.

Do you have any references?

Providing references is a frequent request of inquisitive investors, and for good reason. Make sure you have a system in place to provide them quickly so there isn't a significant lag time between when the potential investor asks and when they're introduced to your references.

Here are a few tips for providing references to an investor:

1. **Identify three of your previous investors as possible references.** First of all, ask them if they're willing and available to act as a reference for your potential investors. Once they agree, schedule a role-play discussion to ask questions about their experience with your firm so that you can ensure they'll give you an excellent review and are well prepared for future conversations.

2. **Ensure that your references are knowledgeable enough so that they can hold a conversation with sophisticated investors who are conducting due diligence on your firm.** This will help assure the potential investor that you're a quality operator who's worth making a bet on. Additionally, your savvier previous investors will be able to speak the language of real estate and know what key points to touch on when conducting these calls, which will quickly alleviate any concerns the potential investor may have.

3. **Make sure your references respond quickly to emails and will actually follow up.** It's a really poor reflection on your business if the potential investor contacts a reference and then hears nothing but crickets. Make sure that you've selected someone who's always responsive to emails and willing to set up calls during the business day. If a potential investor mentions that one of your references never got back to them, don't use them as a reference in the future. Granted, it can be very challenging to identify a previous investor who's the perfect combination of a) accredited, b) sophisticated, and c) not too busy to answer additional emails. This is why #4 on this list is so important.

4. **Each year, individually take each of these three identified references out to dinner as an act of gratitude.** It's always a good idea to thank the people who have helped your business succeed, but references that you can rely on to always answer their phones or emails need to be given special care and thanks. Make them feel valued and don't be afraid to make a few four-money sign reservations on Yelp. Of course, any way you can motivate them to continue to help

you with your process is likely an excellent investment of your resources: think thank-you notes, Amazon gift cards, company swag (that they'll actually use), et cetera.

What happens if there's a natural disaster?

Unfortunately, natural disasters are a risk one takes when investing in real estate. If they invest in enough properties over enough number of years, it's likely that they'll eventually have to deal with some adverse effects of Mother Nature. While we at Asym have been fortunate to avoid major challenges, we've still dealt with our share of fallout from natural disasters. They're never fun. With proper planning, insurance, and risk-management tactics, you can reduce the problems they can cause in the event that something happens. It's important to have all of these in place and be able to let the investors know exactly what your plan looks like.

Here are a few tips for discussing issues related to natural disasters:

1. **Address the reality that the potential of natural disasters is a concern of owning any real estate property.**
2. **Discuss the specifics of the insurance you've selected and how it will protect the asset, as well as them as an investor.** For example, if you purchased insurance for loss of rental income, specifically outline those terms. Investors will find this very reassuring.
3. **If you've specifically avoided certain regions because of their susceptibility to natural disasters, make that clear.** For

example, the Federal Emergency Management Agency (FEMA) ranks locations based on the anticipated frequency of flooding in the area. As a general rule, we don't typically invest in an area designated as greater than a 500-year flood zone (an area with a 1/500 annual chance of a flood). I find that simply adding details like this helps paint a clear picture to the investors that you've thought strategically about mitigating this risk.

4. **If there are explicit reasons why your particular asset class or investment will hold up during a natural disaster, share them with investors.** As an example, the mobile home park business typically isn't as susceptible to flooding as other asset classes because the homes themselves are positioned more than 12 inches off the ground. This can make a significant difference when discussing this specific risk.

How do I know this isn't a Ponzi scheme?

I won't sugar coat it: There's a considerable amount of fraud taking place in the investment world. Savvy investors need assurance that they won't end up on the next episode of *American Greed* on CNBC. As with any questions regarding potential risks, always acknowledge that the concern is valid, particularly as it relates to a passive investor's dependence on the ethical behavior of the operating partner(s). I've found it helpful to walk investors through some of the steps you've taken that specifically address this risk and demonstrate how challenging it would be to disguise an illicit opportunity as legitimate, given the scope of your process.

Here are a few topics to cover when answering the inevitable Ponzi-scheme question:

1. **Discuss portions of your due diligence process that provide cold, hard facts, especially if verified by third parties.** For example, if you pull the title on a property your operating partner claims to own and the title reflects that they in fact do own the property, that would be something any investor would be interested to know.

2. **When you visit the operating partner's currently owned properties, keep your eyes open for situations that confirm the opportunity is authentic and in good standing, then share your perspective with investors.** For example, if you talk to the onsite property manager of one of these properties, and they know the operator well, it would confirm that they frequently visit the asset and are actively involved in its management.

3. **Communicate any ongoing efforts that provide transparency into what's happening at the property level during the hold period.** If you're planning on making additional onsite visits during the hold period, let the potential investor know that you'll not only review the financials and statements provided by the onsite manager, but also personally inspect the property to confirm that its status (occupancy, cleanliness, et cetera) is in line with the quarterly reports.

4. **Mention previous investors who undertook their own extensive independent due diligence process and concluded that everything was in good standing.**

5. **Run a background check and communicate that you have done so to potential investors.**

6. **Discuss possible legal measures that can be taken if you or the operating partner act in bad faith, especially given that you're pooling investors together for the purchase of securities.** As I've mentioned throughout this book, securities violations have serious financial and legal implications. Make sure investors know that if an operator should act improperly, the passive investors will be well-positioned to pursue them in court, given the leverage that the legal system creates when dealing with securities.

What's your track record?

To answer this question as efficiently as possible, it's important to have an easy-to-read document prepared outlining the team's track record in the business. Remember though, if you're just getting started, you'll want to promote your operating partner as the expert, rather than yourself, and therefore, use their track record as opposed to your own. I like to keep this document as simple as possible, with just enough detail to clearly highlight the firm's success.

Here's an example layout of a track record document:

Property Name	Asset Class	Purchase Date	Projected ROI	Performance to Date	Closing Date

I'd also highlight the assets that have been realized (aka taken full cycle) so investors can see that you and your partner have had previous success in fully and successfully implementing the business plan.

Any time you're providing previous track record information, it's imperative that you state that past performance is not indicative of future results, both in the email that you send to the investors and the track record document itself. Treat this suggestion with the same level of importance as recommending that each investor refer to their own CPA and/or attorney prior to making an investment decision. Always remember to do it.

CHAPTER 12

Closing the Sale:
Taking Commitments and
Getting the Deal Funded

O nce you've gone through the investor's due diligence questions and confirmed their thorough understanding of the investment, it's time to close the deal. Your specific closing process may vary based on a variety of other factors, but the key is that you must be intentional about systematizing your process so that you can streamline and optimize it.

OUTLINE YOUR PROCESS

Once you reach the conclusion of the due diligence call, I'd insert something similar to the below into your closing process.

Do you have any additional questions?
No.
Ok great. So, as far as next steps, if you're ready to move forward, [insert your specific process here].

Here's an example of what your specific process could sound like:

We take verbal commitments upfront and then we send out the legal documents. When you complete the documents and return them, your reservation becomes a commitment. Like I mentioned, the verbal commitment deadline is [insert date here] and the funding deadline is [insert date here]. Just so I can plan accordingly, do you have an idea of what amount you anticipate moving forward with?

ESTABLISH FOLLOW-UP DATES AND
THE FINAL DECISION DEADLINE

If the potential investor needs time to think, that's no problem at all. However, you must establish a target date by which point you can follow up. If they say, "I'm actually not sure, do you mind if I talk to my spouse and let you know?" your response should be enthusiastic and agreeable.

For example, you could say, "Absolutely. Please take your time to talk it through. If I don't hear from you in five days, do you mind if I shoot you an email just to confirm either way? That way, we can keep track of our total equity allocation for the close."

This allows investors to opt in to receiving that follow-up email from you (they almost always do), and it establishes a timeline for you to follow up (and hopefully, for them to commit to moving forward). In the event they'd prefer to initiate the follow up, let them know that works for you too.

Establishing a follow-up deadline is absolutely critical to keeping the ball rolling. People who are considering investing in real estate are very frequently successful and busy individuals. Usually, they're passively investing because they don't have the time to be operators, meaning that you'll need to be the one driving the communication ship.

If you feel uncomfortable requesting follow-up dates and communicating accordingly, just remember that you're helping them stay on track with the deal's timeline. No one likes a missed opportunity, and if you've gotten far enough to have a due diligence call, they deserve your willingness to follow up and confirm their status.

Establishing and tracking follow-up deadlines is the only way to create an effective closing process. If you don't establish them throughout the process, you'll be left trying to remember if and when you can follow up with potential investors. This will result in missed opportunities to close deals, and the money of potential investors will remain sitting in their bank accounts earning less than 1% interest.

In addition to outlining your closing process and establishing follow-up deadlines, here are a few things to consider when closing the sale:

1. **Reiterate that the investment is time sensitive and will likely be oversubscribed before the deadline.** This establishes the much-needed time frame, as well as creates urgency for them to take action.

2. **Don't be pushy.** If it's clear they want to get off the phone, don't hesitate to let them do so. You certainly don't want to push someone into a real estate deal. However, it's critical to emphasize the deadline of the offering and request a follow-up date prior to jumping off the call. To clarify, it's ok to push for them to opt in to a follow-up email so that you can either remove them from your communications on this offering or include them in the opportunity. It's not ok to push for an actual investment commitment. That's an important distinction to make here.

3. **If you're taking verbal investment reservations and requesting the capital later, and the investor is considering between a range of amounts, always suggest they reserve the larger amount (as long as they're comfortable with it).** There are several reasons for this. Most importantly, investors need to get in the habit of reserving the larger amount, so they have the opportunity to invest the amount they actually want to. Once a deal is oversubscribed, they won't be able to add to their investment amount, but they can always reduce it. Here's the thing: You'll likely be able to replace their capital commitment with another investor. From an

administrative perspective, you want to keep the number of investors as low as possible, so having them commit to larger amounts is preferable. (Bonus: People have the tendency to fund their larger amount if they verbalize it.)

4. **Express gratitude if they confirm over the phone that they're moving forward.** Let them know how much it means that they've entrusted you with their capital, regardless of the investment amount, and how seriously you take that responsibility. When an investor commits to moving forward, take a quick moment to mention not only that you're really excited about this offering, but also that you look forward to delivering on the opportunity so that you two can continue to work together well into the future.

5. **Once an investor has confirmed their intent to move forward, clearly outline the next steps they'll take to complete their investment and then email them a supplemental "Investor Instructions Document" that restates what you've outlined on the call.** Having an easy-to-read document will make it much easier on the investor and further establishes your credibility because the systemization of this process implies you've done it over and over again. Also, visual learners might unintentionally tune out on the phone and need a written document to clearly follow along.

Having helped hundreds of investors through the commitment process, I can tell you that the more times you do this, the more natural it'll become. Even real estate rookies will be in good shape using this list as a starting point, as potential investors will be assured they're making a bet on a team with plenty of experience under its belt.

Once the commitments have been established, the next part of the process is the legal document execution, the issuance of wire instructions, and the confirmation of the receipt of funds.

Below are a few tips that can help move this process along without any major hiccups:

1. **Provide the legal documents via an electronic document signing platform.** Private placement memorandums can be anywhere from 100-220 pages. Don't burden the investor with having to print out these documents in order to sign them. It's critical that you use DocuSign (www.docusign. com) or one of its competitors to alleviate the challenges associated with this task. This will also help with your record-keeping process.

2. **Provide the funding instructions (and any sensitive documents) via an encrypted email client such as SendInc** (www.sendinc.com) or through Gmail's encrypted email feature. Make the investor aware you'll be sending this information through an encrypted service so they know it isn't spam, as it might appear differently on their end. Confirm that any future wire instructions will be sent from a similar encrypted email platform, and if they ever have any questions about the validity of the wire instructions, they should contact you immediately.

3. **Unless investors have a genuine reason for not sending a wire or an Automatic Clearing House (AHC), require that they do so.** There's nothing more frustrating than dealing with issues related to a lost check in the mail. (You'd be shocked to find out how frequently this happens.) To nip

these issues in the bud, we stopped giving out our mailing address for funding.

4. **Check your receiving bank account for the funds daily and confirm receipt with the investor within that business day.** Put yourself in the investor's shoes: From the time they send an enormous amount of investment capital to you to the time you confirm receipt, their hard-earned money is in no man's land. I understand that checking a bank account can be time consuming, so I suggest granting an administrative assistant viewing access to the bank account so they can confirm when the funds are received.

Your success in the real estate business will be heavily dependent on repeat customers. I'll circle back to this in Chapter 15: Paving the Road to $450,000 in Annual Income, but here's the bottom line: An investor's propensity to reinvest will be contingent on their experience all the way through the finish line, and the best way to scale your business is to work with the same top-quality investors over and over. The post-investment portion of your business needs to be handled with just as much professionalism and care as your initial outreach.

Here are a few tips to help ensure this experience is top notch.

1. **Send a thank-you note immediately after you receive their funds.** Buying and designing a few thank-you notes is one of the best investments you can make, as they ensure this next phase of the relationship with your investors starts off on the right foot, and they cost almost nothing.

2. **After the investment has been made, communicate with the investors consistently.** Once you've established a post-investment communication schedule, you have to stick to it. Consistency is more important here than anything else. For example, quarterly reports should be issued within the same few days every single quarter.

3. **End every quarterly report with an invitation for investors to reach out with any questions.** Knowing that they have an open line of communication with you, the person they invested with, goes a long way.

4. **Always answer emails from investors within 24 hours.** If you don't have the capacity to grant this level of service, hire someone to handle the task or to free up your time so that you do.

5. **Invite investors to reconnect with you during the investment.** We reach out to investors bi-annually to check in and see what they find most compelling in the investment space, as well as provide them with our outlook on the future and the investments we anticipate will become available. These conversations frequently uncover important information and unquestionably result in a more meaningful relationship between us and our investors. Better relationships equal investors making more frequent investments, as well as higher average investment amounts.

6. **Send gifts to your high-dollar investors annually.** Every year, we send a special branded gift to investors who have invested above a certain dollar amount with us in the previous calendar year. We usually have a budget of $20-$50 for these gifts, which have included things like

branded hot/cold cups, wireless chargers, and a variety of small but useful items. We purchase our branded material from Creative Marketing Concepts (www.creativemc.com) or one of its competitors.

These steps will certainly help ensure you start off your relationships with your new investors on the right foot, as well as maintain them through the investment process. Of course, regardless of whether or not you complete the steps above, an investor's experience with you is most importantly dictated by the performance of their investments. If you routinely raise capital for offerings that don't perform, you aren't going to succeed in the real estate business. Since I'm here to explain the capital raising side of the business, I won't go into great detail about ways in which you can work to ensure your investments perform, but I wanted to emphasize that this should always be top of mind when you think of solidifying relationships with your investors.

CHAPTER 13

Challenging Situations and What to Do About Them

D espite the extent of upfront due diligence conducted, you'll likely face some obstacles in your real estate career. After all, you're investing in real property with real people in the real world, so the unexpected is bound to happen. Especially if you build a large firm with investments across multiple entities, states, and asset classes, you'll unquestionably receive, and be required to send, some unfortunate communications.

No one likes to receive negative information, especially when it comes to investment capital, nor does anyone want to be the bearer of bad news that will likely cause a negative reaction from their investor base. With that in mind, it's worth taking some time to prepare for this situation and create a system by which to handle challenging issues.

If you're going to work in this space, here are a few examples of problems that might come up during any investment:

- A natural disaster damaged the investment property.
- Cash flow is significantly reduced or non-existent for a quarter.
- Incorrect information was provided to the investor.
- A significant change happened during escrow, negatively impacting the return profile of the offering.
- An anchor tenant decided to move out unexpectedly.

Regardless of how detailed and focused you are, if you're involved in enough deals over a long enough time period, you'll likely face some or all of these problems. The key of this chapter to help you unlock the best ways to tackle these issues, keep your cool, and mitigate any damage they might cause.

THE CHALLENGING DECISION ALGORITHM

One way to mitigate these challenges *before* they come up is to run every major decision in your business through what I call **The Challenging Decision Algorithm**. The algorithm is simple, to the point, and will always guide you in the right direction. Ready for it? Before making a decision ask yourself: "What's in the investors' best interest over the long term?" Whatever the answer is to that question is the way in which you should address the decision.

The algorithm has two important parts: 1) the investors' best interest and 2) the long-term outcome. The first part of the algorithm is very straightforward and has been a reoccurring theme throughout this book. The business should be set up from top to bottom to make sure you're profoundly aligned with your investors. You and your key team members' compensation should be heavily weighted on performance, and the windfall of your compensation should only come after investors have received their preferred return and a return of capital. Many problems can arise when you're not financially incentivized to act on your investors' best interest, so set these parameters from the start.

The second part of the algorithm is not as straightforward. When I first started Asym Capital, I was hell-bent on making sure that the administrative fees paid by investors were extremely low. This way, I could pass as much cash flow as possible directly to their bank accounts. However, I eventually realized that this thinking was incomplete. In my early days, if there was a CPA that would file the tax return of one of our offerings for $1,500 versus a CPA that would cost closer to $5,000, I'd always assume that the cheaper option was better for the investors. The thought here was that the $3,500 in savings would go directly into the investors' pockets. Clearly, that was in their best interest, right? Unsurprisingly, there's a reason the cheaper CPA was only charging $1,500. When it comes to something as critical as your firm's accounting processes, it's especially important that you aren't being short-sighted or shallow-pocketed in your view of what's best.

Another example is the fee structure you set up for yourself and your firm. Again, back in the early days of Asym Capital, our fee structure was so streamlined that, at one point, there was frequently a 0% assets-under-management fee during our hold period. What could be more investor-favorable than 0% in fees? That was the short-term view talking. This structure will pigeonhole your business in a way that keeps you from providing the level of service you want, especially if you begin to scale. Sure, a 0% assets-under-management fee might make sense when you can answer every phone call and email yourself, but what about when you need to focus on conducting due diligence on another offering? In order for you to take on an additional team member, you'd have to pay out of pocket, either limiting the quality of your firm's investor relations or limiting the quality of due diligence you can conduct on new offerings. Both are unacceptable. This is why it's so important to be mindful of your long-term trajectory when making important business decisions, such as your fee structure or who to hire.

WHEN THINGS ACTUALLY GO WRONG

The Challenging Decision Algorithm will help you avoid a lot of the major issues that real estate firms typically face, but something will eventually slip through the cracks, and there are always ways to learn from new challenges as they're presented.

Here are a few more suggestions for handling issues as they arise:

1. **If an area of your business is struggling, hire a team member who can provide an appropriate level of support.** There's nothing I dislike more than when an operator is in the

process of raising a significant amount of capital and can't get back to an investor's questions within 24 hours. Say, for example, they're raising $10,000,000 with a 2% upfront fee. That equates to $200,000 in upfront revenue. A portion of that income could be put towards hiring an investor relations team member to take care of investors during the hold period. As you know from reading this book, I'm obsessed with efficiency and hate wasting money—but I don't pinch pennies when it comes to investor experience. Stinginess and greed can be deadly in this business, and for good reason. Don't try to keep all of the proceeds for yourself. That is a short-sighted way of operating a business and will always cost you in the end.

2. **Do everything you can to protect the investors' capital.** For those of you who weren't in the game (or watching the news) in 2008, it was a bloodbath. Many experienced operators with decades in the business struggled to make mortgage payments and keep their properties in good standing. I know a lot of operators who did everything they could to ensure investors' capital was preserved, but none is more pronounced this one: A large multi-family property operator, whom I know personally, was facing foreclosure if an asset wasn't recapitalized. Some might argue that the asset was overleveraged, but the loan-to-value ratio (loan amount / value of asset) was well within industry standards at the time. The problem was the market they were invested in collapsed by nearly 40%, and the liquidity in the sector completely dried up. Despite making consistent payments on their debt, the loan was coming due and

the bank required an additional $1,000,000 or the asset was going to be foreclosed. After contemplating for a few weeks, the operator made the decision to pay out of pocket to save the property from foreclosure. He literally wrote a personal check for $1,000,000. This was incredibly admirable, yes, but more than anything it should tell you how seriously they took the protection of the investors' capital. After the rebound of multi-family valuations in the area, the property was sold and the proceeds of the sale was substantial enough to repay the operating partner, as well as provide a healthy return to investors. However, at the time the check was originally written, it was unclear at best that this would happen. Since those days, this particular sponsor's firm has grown massively and now owns more than 10,000 units. The investors from that previous deal are investors for life, as they should be. This isn't just a one-off example; there are many stories like this from that era. While it might not be possible for you to write a check for $1,000,000 right now, just ensure that you're going into each investment with the mindset that you'll do anything to protect investor capital, prior to and during the entire lifespan of each investment.

3. **Face challenges head on, be transparent about them, and always come to investors with a solution.** If a major issue arises, focus your attention on the matter, learn everything you can about the situation, identify a solution, and establish an estimated timeline during which the matter will be resolved, all prior to contacting investors. This way, when they receive the unfortunate information, it'll be clear that

you're already working to handle the issue and have set a potential resolution timeline. Should your proposed resolution require them to vote (for example, if the resolution involves taking on additional capital), clearly outline your perspective, including what your preferred vote outcome looks like? Remember, most passive investors are focused on their non-real estate jobs. Bring a solution to them and ensure the decision-making process is as easy as possible.

KEY TAKEAWAYS FROM DEALING WITH A MASSIVE INVESTOR RELATIONS HEADACHE

In 2017, we purchased three properties for one of our funds, the last of which closed near year-end. Right after the close of the final property, the seller went dark and stopped all communication with us and our partners. Normally, this wouldn't be much of a problem, but we needed information about the close in order to file our taxes.

Typically, during tax season, CPA firms prioritize their clients based on importance and necessity. In this instance, the seller wasn't pressing their CPA firm to make it a priority, as they had already received their funds from the sale. Furthermore, the seller had just sold us their last property, so we couldn't even try to act like we might be interested in buying another asset from them if they gave us the information we were looking for. We simply had zero leverage.

It became increasingly clear that this had the potential to create a massive headache for us and our investors, and as the tax deadline edged closer, we realized we were going to need to extend our tax returns for the fund.

It was time to face this reality, so we sent out an initial email to all investors notifying them that, due to the challenges we were having with the seller, they would likely need to file an extension. Then there was another delay as the seller continued to be unresponsive, and then another.

This situation was the bane of my existence for several months. Every day, I'd wake up fearing that I'd receive another email from investors requesting an update on the situation, even though we were notifying them every time we had any information to share. From an investor relations standpoint, it was very challenging.

In all fairness, it's somewhat common for investors in syndications to need to extend their return, but if you have a significant number of investors who are just getting started in the process of diversifying into the world of passive syndications, they'll likely not be accustomed to filing after the initial deadline. This was the circumstance I was in at the time, and the reactions of the investors ranged from slightly disgruntled to extremely frustrated.

While this story isn't nearly as bad as some of the potential challenges you may face in real estate, any problematic situation is a chance to show your investors what kind of person you are and who they're actually dealing with. View issues like this as (hopefully) rare opportunities to prove that you're embodying the values that you discussed while courting them as investors.

Here are some of the key takeaways we learned when dealing with this challenge, which are applicable to any issues that might arise:

1. **Respond quickly to investor questions.** Any time an investor asked a question about this topic, we made an extra effort to respond as quickly as possible, regardless of what we were doing. I know, this isn't in line with my task-batching suggestions at the beginning of the book, but this was the highest priority. When dealing with issues like this, the goal is investor retention, as opposed to focusing efforts on attracting new investors. This tip alone will significantly reduce the amount of backlash you'll face when dealing with any serious investor relations problem.

2. **Set communication timelines and stick to them.** While the matter is getting resolved, set timelines for future communications and keep them no matter what. Many times, when things go wrong, issues aren't able to be resolved as quickly as you originally anticipate that they might. Don't set an estimated timeline for the matter to be handled and then just let it pass. No one likes to be the bearer of bad news, but if you set the expectation that you'll update investors by a certain date, they should receive an email that morning, even if the update isn't what you were hoping to give them.

3. **Take responsibility.** Even if you didn't directly create the challenge, recognize that your investors put trust in you to handle all of the problems related to the investment. Take responsibility, own it, and sympathize with them, but

don't throw yourself under the bus and do not communicate panic. Investors want to know that you're taking the concern extremely seriously, but they also want to know that you have everything under control. Any correspondence on the topic should cover all of the following:

    a. *We understand that this has been a challenge for you.*

    b. *This is our top priority right now.*

    c. *Here are the remedies we have put in place to resolve the matter.*

    d. *Here are the systems we have put in place to mitigate this issue in the future.*

4. **Identify the cause of the issue and make the necessary changes to ensure that similar problems are mitigated or eliminated in the future.** While tax timelines are always a challenge in the syndicated space, going forward, we made an extra effort to confirm certain communication timelines via email with all of our sellers to create more leverage in the event that they go dark after the close. We also hired an outsourced CPA-licensed CFO that's well-equipped to resolve any future time-sensitive matters related to taxes.

This list probably took you five minutes to read, but there's so much to learn from these simple suggestions. Based on my experience, fewer than 10% of the businesses in the U.S. operate within these guidelines. If you deal with challenging situations as outlined above, your investors will immediately notice the difference between the way you address these kinds of issues compared to your competitors.

Thankfully, after we incessantly followed up with the seller for months and eventually threatened legal action, the seller finally provided us the necessary information, and our investors were able to file their returns. While some of the investors in this deal likely found the experience a pain, anyone paying attention to our communications knew how seriously we took the situation and that all other business initiatives were put second on the priority list until the matter was resolved. Savvy investors will likely view this experience as a good sign, in terms of the way we might address even more challenging situations in the future, should they arise.

PUT YOURSELF IN A POSITION TO DELIVER FOR YOUR OPERATING PARTNER

Being successful in the real estate investment business requires a commitment to acting in the best long-term interest of both your investors and the partners you work with. Real estate entrepreneurs who are focused on the short term usually don't make it very far in the business and rarely survive even a modest economic correction. One point where it's absolutely critical to remember this is when you're establishing an investment reservation amount with your operating partner.

If you're completing a capital raise for an operating partner, you'll most likely face this daunting question that every capital raiser has asked themselves at least once: "Should I shoot for the moon and claim that I can raise a substantial amount of money, or do I remain conservative to ensure I can deliver on my promises?"

If you're thinking to yourself that the answer is clearly the latter, I can promise you it's much easier said than done. Once you start actually calculating the proceeds you might miss out on if you drastically *underestimate* your ability to raise capital, you'll start to realize why so many are tempted to inflate their abilities and then end up coming up short.

Having said that, when an operating partner is about to close a property that requires a certain amount of investment capital, that capital better show up to the pre-determined bank account when needed, or the closing could be delayed and the entire deal could blow up. This is completely unacceptable. Conversely, it's also probably going to really hurt your pocket if you only reserve $1,000,000 for your raise and end up with an additional $4,000,000 of commitments sitting uninvested on the sidelines. Both of these situations would be unfortunate, so it's important to create a system to balance these two extremes and mitigate their respective risks.

In order to accomplish this, you need to be able to clearly communicate your funding commitments with your operating partner.

Here are two terms I think are important to define upfront and then use during the investment commitment process:

1. **Reservation.** This is a verbal reservation of an investment amount that's usually pending further actions, such as your continued due diligence, feedback from your investor base, et cetera. In short, this reservation is subject to change. For example, if an offering requires $10,000,000 of equity and you reserve $2,000,000, you're reserving

the right to raise that $2,000,000 and only $8,000,000 is left to be accounted for.

2. **Investment commitment.** This is a true commitment to fund a specific dollar amount on a specific date. Once this has been established, your operating partner(s) will rely on you to deliver and failing to do so will likely have significant consequences. Depending on the deal, there could even be legal implications for failing to fund your investment commitment amount.

When discussing your capital raise's estimated outcome with your operating partner, I suggest breaking it down into these three categories:

1. **Realistic projection.** This is the actual estimate of the equity amount you believe you'll raise, given your current understanding of the offering and its potential reception from your investors. When discussing your realistic projection, be sure to take into account the offering's alignment with your brand and the educational material you've provided to your investor base.

2. **Stretch goal.** This is the equity amount you anticipate raising if everything during the raise is executed flawlessly and your offering is well-received by your investor base. If the operating partner is open to it, I like to establish an investment reservation of our stretch goal early in the process. Then, if we need to reduce it later when the operating partner needs a firm commitment, we can always do so. This

provides maximum flexibility without putting ourselves or our operating partner in a precarious situation.

3. **Worst-case scenario.** This would be the total capital amount committed by your investors if the raise doesn't go as planned, and the response is nowhere near what you originally anticipated. Essentially, this is the number where you think *I genuinely can't see it being lower than this.*

By structuring your conversation with your operating partner as such, they'll see the full spectrum of your perspective on the anticipated outcome without leaving too much opportunity on the table.

Having said that, accurately estimating the equity investment and communicating it effectively is only one important part of the process. You also need to be crystal clear on the timeline, specifically the date on which the operating partner needs a firm commitment. I like to think of this as the "point of no return."

Here are a few key questions to ask the operating partner in regard to the commitment timeline:

1. How much flexibility is there for the amount of money you (the capital raiser) can raise? For example, if you reserve a significant investment amount and later reduce it, how problematic will this be, in terms of closing the property, and at what date does that become problematic?
2. At what date does your investment reservation need to be solidified as an investment commitment?
3. What are the consequences if you're unable to deliver the capital once you've made a firm commitment?

Not only would I have this discussion upfront, but I'd do so via email so that you both can refer back to it later. I'd also check in again on these three key questions as the weeks progress and see if the answers shifted at all during the investment process. I can't stress this enough. This mutual understanding—or lack thereof—holds the potential to make or break the entire opportunity, as well as a relationship with an operating partner. Don't take this lightly. It may be a bit uncomfortable getting into this level of detail, but it's critical. Do it upfront and continue to check in as the closing deadline approaches.

This level of specificity sets clear guidelines, yes, but the reason that it's such an important conversation is because there's significant variance out there about just how much of a problem it'll be if you come up short.

For example, if the operating partner has a significant amount of flexibility and could raise $1,000,000 on their own very quickly, you could "reserve" $1,000,000, then give it your all to meet that number. If you came up short, it wouldn't cause too much disruption because the operating partner could easily fill the gap.

In other circumstances, any gap at all could put you and your operating partner in dire straits. True story: I know an operating partner who worked with a crowdfunding portal that reserved $500,000 for a close. The crowdfunding portal ended up having a fairly successful raise and received $450,000, only $50,000 shy. However, the crowdfunding company failed to communicate their underperformance until the 11th hour and, given the timing of the close, it became a huge problem for the operating partner and ultimately led to severed ties between the two parties.

As a business owner, you don't want to limit your growth by establishing an investment reservation that doesn't grant interested investors access to the deal. On the other hand, it's absolutely critical that you have a reputation of being able to deliver on your promises. Be transparent with the operating partner and ensure that you're both on the same page throughout the capital raising process.

Here's an example of an email one of our operating partners might receive in the initial stages of a raise:

We anticipate raising a total of somewhere in the $3,000,000–$5,000,000 range. We have a stretch goal of $5,000,000 and would like to reserve that amount, which will be solidified as an investment commitment on [insert date]. Is that amount of flexibility still ok at this point? Could you please confirm that the commitment deadline of [insert date] still works on your end?

Then, as the raise continues, we keep the operating partner in the know and eventually establish a firm commitment amount on the date we agreed upon.

Once that firm commitment has been established, we're locked in as a company to do anything it takes to ensure that we get to that number. If we commit to a number and it looks like we're going to come up short, we'll exhaust any means necessary to get the equity needed to ensure our reputation is maintained. Even if this means selling personal investments, the wire that we send out will be exactly what we committed to—and not a dollar less. Our reputation and our word are everything. That's how you should think of it as well.

Always be hyper-conservative in your first few raises, especially if there are any negative consequences whatsoever for coming up short.

Let's say that you have a stretch goal of $1,000,000, a realistic goal of $500,000, and a worst-case scenario of $250,000. If the operating partner has zero flexibility and needs a commitment amount from you upfront, just go with the $250,000. Trust me. Any high-quality operating partner who's worth their salt now will be worth their salt for many years to come. If you earn the reputation of executing on your promises, you'll be able to work with them in the future, and the additional $750,000 you might have been able to raise on that first deal will be completely trivial after a few more transactions.

CHAPTER 14

How to Be Compensated for Raising Money

At this point in the book, you should understand that staying within the formal guidelines of the world of securities can be challenging, but it's also absolutely crucial. This will likely be the case at all stages in your career as a real estate entrepreneur. The regulatory hurdles proportionally increase as the scope and scale of your business grows. If you've decided to be in this space in a meaningful way, you have to learn to respect the rules.

When it comes to raising capital for real estate, the main thing you want to avoid doing without a license is raising money for a deal in which you're not a member of the General Partner (GP) but are being compensated by the GP (a third party) for capital raising duties. This would violate broker-dealer laws because you'd be acting as a "broker," as opposed to an "issuer."

I've read through thousands of pages of legal documents and reviewed case law with a fine-tooth comb. When it comes to securities, the reality is you can't be compensated for brokering them without a license. The best and most common way to overcome this challenge is to become a member of the GP and a fully integrated partner of the firm, one who's assisting the firm in ways other than just raising money. This will allow you to avoid the challenges associated with most of the securities laws that surround this topic. Of course, there are significant implications associated with being a member of the GP. You'd be considered part of the team that's overseeing the entire investment and, to some extent, be potentially responsible for its outcome. Even so, due to complications surrounding securities law, it's the most popular way to act as a capital raiser in the real estate sector.

If you're not interested in becoming a member of the GP, another potential option is to create your own investing entity and receive the compensation created at the investing entity level. This would avoid the issues with receiving third-party compensation, as the investors in your entity would be compensating you directly. I'll describe this structure in more detail below. Of course, there are many important nuances and gray areas with all of these options, so always consult your attorney prior to finalizing your legal structure.

PARTNERING WITH AN OPERATING PARTNER

In order to avoid the challenges associated with third-party compensation, becoming an operator is the most streamlined and common approach to raising capital for real estate. If you're able to identify a firm with a solid track record but is also in need of additional investor capital, it could be worth your time to consider fully integrating with them and joining their firm.

Partnering with an Operator

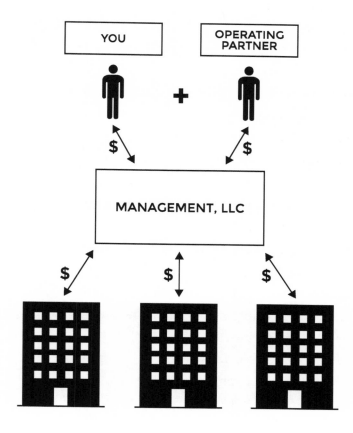

While these partnerships can take a variety of different shapes and sizes, I'll start with the basics. Let's say you identify a firm that's looking for a partner who can handle a litany of duties, in addition to bringing significant equity to the table when it's time to close. They agree to take you on as a partner and compensate you by providing you 25% of the proceeds paid to the GP for any deal in which you're involved.

The compensation to the GP is provided via the waterfall split, which describes how the investment's proceeds are paid, when it's paid, and whom it's paid to. Let's say, for example, that the waterfall split outlines an 8% preferred return with a 70/30 (investor/GP) split thereafter. The preferred return here implies that the passive investors/limited partners (LPs) will receive an 8% annual return on their investment prior to the GP participating in the proceeds of the split. If you agree to join the GP in order to participate in 25% of its proceeds, this would imply that you'd participate in 25% of the 30% that the GP is entitled to.

Calculating the Return to Investors

Continuing with the example above, let's assume that the property you're raising capital for is anticipated to produce a 22% gross annualized return (prior to the waterfall split).

Here's how to calculate the return to the investors:

- 22% (gross annualized return) - 8% (preferred return) = 14% annualized remaining to be split up 70/30
- 14% * 70% = 9.8% annualized

- 8% (preferred return) + 9.8% (net of the 70/30 split) = 17.8% annualized return net to investors

Calculating the Compensation to the GP

Here's how to calculate the compensation to the GP for the same deal:

- 22% (gross annualized return) - 8% (preferred return) = 14% annualized remaining to be split up 70/30
- 14% * 30% = 4.2% annualized net to the GP
- 4.2% * 25% (capital raising partner) = 1.05% annualized net to you, the capital raiser

For example, if this deal required $2,000,000 in equity, you'd anticipate receiving an average of $21,000 annually for each year the property was held. So, if it was a seven-year hold, you could expect to receive a total of $147,000 over the duration of the investment. Keep in mind that the windfall of the compensation will likely be provided to you in year seven, once the property is sold.

While market dynamics are always changing, this is a fairly reasonable assumption.

However (and this is the really important part), this calculation assumes the property performs. You may remember that I've constantly reiterated throughout this book just how essential it is for you to identify an operating partner who can deliver on the promises they make to their investors. This is why.

Enumerating Your Duties

In order for this structure to be compliant with the SEC, you'd need to be a genuine partner of the GP who's bringing more to the table than just equity. However, it's important that you not only complete other non-capital raising tasks for the firm, but you also need to clearly outline your additional duties in writing to ensure you're buttoned up in terms of these securities requirements.

Non-capital raising duties may include:

1. Due diligence
2. Investor relations
3. Fund administration
4. Issuance and preparation of tax documents and quarterly reports
5. Preparation of marketing materials
6. Consulting services related to
   a. Deal structure
   b. Legal document drafting
   c. Overall investment strategy
   d. A variety of other duties

By clearly outlining your duties in a formal agreement, you'll have a paper trail proving your status as a bona fide partner of the firm, as opposed to a third party who's simply raising money for an opportunity they're not otherwise associated with.

CREATING A FUND OF FUNDS

Another potential structure for raising capital is to pool all of your investors into an investment entity ("fund of funds") that then invests into the GP's investment opportunity. This way, you can receive compensation that's paid by your investment entity to you directly, avoiding any broker-dealer laws. In this situation, the operating partner is simply the recipient of your funds and wouldn't be paying you to raise money. In fact, in many cases, the operating partner may not pay you anything at all, since your compensation is being derived at your fund of funds/investment entity level.

Please refer to the following page to review the organizational flowchart.

Fund of Funds

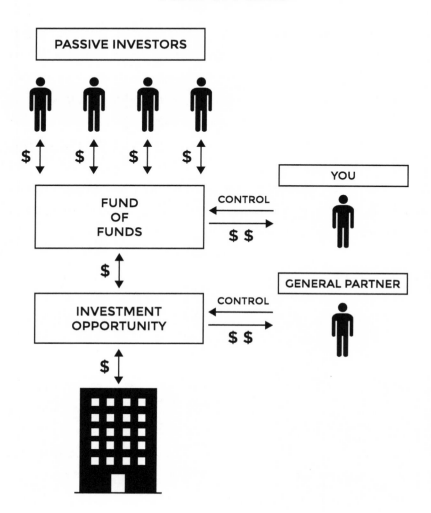

Here's how this structure could work:

Let's say your investors agree to allow you to receive 20% of the proceeds distributed to the investing entity as compensation for your sourcing the deal and making it available to them.

Using the same example above to compare apples to apples, let's assume there's a property that's going to produce a 22% gross annualized return at the property level, and the waterfall structure is the same 8% preferred return with a 70/30 (investor/GP) split thereafter. As discussed above, this would result in a 17.8% annualized return to the **fund of funds entity** that you created. Remember, you're not a member of the GP in this structure, so at this point, I've not yet factored in your compensation.

Here's how to calculate your compensation as a fund of funds manager, assuming the 80/20 (fund of funds investor/capital raiser) split:

- 17.8% annualized return to the fund of funds * 80% = 14.24% annualized net to your investors
- 17.8% annualized return to the fund of funds * 20% = 3.56% annualized net to you, the capital raiser

In this instance, the fund of funds entity would receive a 17.8% annualized return on its investment. Of that 17.8% annualized return, 80% will go to your investors, meaning your investors would receive 14.24% annualized, and you (the capital raiser) would receive 20% of that 17.8%, equating to 3.56% annualized based on how much capital your fund of funds entity invested.

This would mean if you raised that same $2,000,000, you'd expect to receive an average of $71,200 annually during the hold period, or a total of $498,400 over a seven-year period.

With that said, there's an additional layer of splits taking place, which may cause pushback from your investor base.

However, many changes can be made to rectify that. Because you're pooling multiple investors together and, therefore, investing a significant sum of money, you could negotiate more favorable terms from the operator for your fund of funds entity, such as a more advantageous waterfall split. For example, instead of the original 8% preferred return with a 70/30 split, let's say the operating partner would offer your fund of funds entity a 10% preferred return with a 75/25 split if you were able to invest above a certain investment amount. This would increase the investors' net result, even when factoring in your additional compensation at the fund of funds entity level.

Let's first take a look at the proceeds that would be paid to the fund of funds entity in the example immediately above:

- 22% (gross annual return) – 10% (preferred return) = 12% annualized remaining to be split 75/25
- 12% * 75% = 9%
- 10% (preferred return) + 9% (net of split) = 19% annualized return net to the fund of funds entity

Here's how to calculate the returns, net to both your investors and you (the capital raiser), assuming the 80/20 (investor/capital raiser) split:

- 19% annualized return to the fund of funds * 80% = 15.2% annualized net to your investors
- 19% annualized return to the fund of funds * 20% = 3.8% annualized net to you, the capital raiser

As you can see, this would result in the returns to the fund of funds entity increasing from 17.8% to 19%. If you, the capital raiser, were to receive 20% of the proceeds, you'd receive 3.8% annualized (20% of 19%), and the fund of funds investors would receive 15.2% annualized (80% of 19%). A return profile of 15.2% annualized is quite desirable for a passive investor who wouldn't have had access to the opportunity otherwise.

If an 80/20 split on gains at the fund of funds entity level is too steep for your investor base, you could always create a 90/10 or 95/5 split to reduce the fees paid to the capital raiser. The structure itself doesn't necessarily mean that it'll be better or worse from a net-to-investor perspective. The appropriate compensation structure here will be dependent on your investor base, how desirable the investment is, and how much value you're bringing to the table.

Before moving on from this topic, I want to note that while this strategy would avoid common SEC broker-dealer issues, if you utilize this structure for your offerings, it's likely that you'll eventually cross into Registered Investment Advisor (RIA) territory. Because you're no longer investing directly in real estate, but are directing investment into another security, it could be required that you become an RIA. If you pursue this strategy, the federal government requires that you register as an RIA if you have $100,000,000 or more under management (of invested capital). Every state has its own requirements as well. Make sure to consult with your attorney before making this decision, as each state's underlying laws can vary significantly.

BECOMING A LICENSED SECURITIES BROKER

Looking for another option? You could also acquire and maintain the license of a registered broker-dealer or use an existing one. This strategy will allow you to get directly compensated for raising capital as a third party and would not require you to be a member of the GP. As you probably assume, there are some strings attached here as well. Acquiring your own broker-dealer license is incredibly burdensome and requires a series of formal tests and ongoing maintenance to ensure you're in good standing. Even if that doesn't deter you, the upfront fees might. In fact, I know a firm that spent more than $1,000,000 in order to become a licensed broker-dealer. This doesn't even include the rolling annual fees associated with maintaining the license and other compliance issues.

If you want to go the broker-dealer route, a much more common strategy is to leverage another firm's existing broker-dealer license. From a structural standpoint, the licensee/broker-dealer relationship is similar to the structure within real estate sales. When buying a property, a real estate agent is required to have a license, but they're also required to have all of their transactions take place under the umbrella of a broker, which is a higher-level and more involved license.

In this structure, you (the capital raiser) would typically need a Series 7 or Series 82 license, which would allow you to interface directly with potential investors and "sell" securities to them. However, even with that license, you'll still need a registered broker-dealer to help facilitate the transaction.

Because of the associated upfront and maintenance costs with operating a broker-dealer firm, these companies that allow capital raisers to use their higher-level license charge an arm and a leg for the service they provide. While it can vary significantly from company to company, you should expect to pay a flat fee of $10,000-$25,000 (or more) per year, in addition to 10-20% of the compensation you receive for selling securities.

For most people who are just getting started, this is a deal killer. However, if you truly are resistant to formally integrating with an operating partner and becoming a member of the GP, and you don't want to utilize some version of the fund of funds structure, this is certainly something to consider. Of course, it doesn't feel good to know that you're always going to be paying another firm, but being in violation of securities law has significant implications, including (but not limited to) the potential for criminal liability.

OTHER STRUCTURES FOR COMPENSATION

When it comes to operating in the real estate world, I've seen people do everything under the sun, many times with little regard for the formal regulations surrounding securities. Even with the best intentions, the overwhelming burden that federal and state governments have put on those working in the real estate investment sector makes it very challenging to operate within the guidelines, especially if you're a small firm or a solopreneur. As a result, the sector is filled with people attempting to sidestep these rules with varying degrees of aggressiveness.

The reality is that when times are good, those who are aggressive tend to remain unscathed because very few investors are inclined to complain while their investments are performing well. However, the moment that something goes awry with an investment, those who lose money scramble and try to sue anyone and everyone. Unsurprisingly, securities violations make great targets for attorneys who are looking for a potentially lucrative legal angle to put pressure on the operator of an under-performing deal.

We live in an incredibly litigious society. It's always advisable to stay within the formal guidelines when it comes to securities law and consult with your attorney before making any decisions regarding what would be best for you and your firm.

CHAPTER 15

Paving the Road to $450,000 in Annual Income

By 2016, not only had I built up a widespread network of some extremely influential people in the real estate sector, I also had the opportunity to work directly with them. Through Asym Capital, we'd already invested millions of dollars and were seeing consistent proof that our systems and processes were working, as our track record continued to be solidified. I'd also spent more than $100,000 on legal fees creating private placement memorandums and navigating the waters of unregistered securities. Essentially, I created something of value and had extensive knowledge about a topic that had the potential to be extremely lucrative.

When someone suggested that I start a podcast, I was very interested. I also, admittedly, had some reservations about "giving away" free content, exposing a potentially large listener base to my network, and revealing information that I'd worked so hard for years to uncover. However, I quickly overcame my aversion to publicizing my secrets when I completed a simple goal-setting exercise, during which I calculated what I'd need to do to receive $450,000 in income as a real estate entrepreneur.

The reason I decided to focus on $450,000 is that if I was to make $450,000 annually, I'd be securely in the top 1% of income earners in the United States as of 2019. Granted, that might not be enough income for you to live out your wildest dreams, but it would certainly be something pretty remarkable.

As of 2019, there are more than 12,000,000 households that qualify as accredited investors.[6] As a reminder, an accredited investor is an individual who has a net worth of $1,000,000 or has made $200,000 per year over the last two years, or a married couple who cumulatively have a net worth of $1,000,000 or have made $300,000 per year over the last two years.

Let's keep it as straightforward as possible and assume that, on a given capital raise, you'd expect to receive 2% of the capital raised upfront and an average of 1% of the capital raised per year based on the real estate's performance.

Here are the numbers if you have 100 investors each making an investment of $50,000:

- **100 investors x $50,000 per investment = $5,000,000**
- **2% upfront fee = $100,000**
- **1% average annual performance fee during hold period = $50,000 per year**

---

6 www.dqydj.com/accredited-investors-in-america

Assuming a five-year hold period, you'd expect to receive a total of **$350,000** of income from this raise over the duration of the investment. Yes, the $100,000 upfront fee is enough to keep the lights on, but the additional performance bonus is where you really start to generate wealth for yourself.

But here's the important part: If you're working with accredited investors who have the financial means to invest with you again and again, would it be reasonable to assume that they could invest another $50,000 the following year as well?

Now, let's say you continue to implement the lead-nurturing strategies outlined previously in this book and continue to grow your investor base from 100 investors to 200, each of whom is investing $50,000 per year.

- **200 investors x $50,000 per investment = $10,000,000**
- **2% upfront fee = $200,000**
- **1% average annual performance fee during hold period = $100,000 per year**

Assuming a five-year hold period, you'd expect to receive a total of **$700,000** of income from this raise. Yes, that's correct. If you're able to raise $10,000,000 with the compensation structure outlined above, you're likely going to receive $700,000 of cumulative income during the hold period, assuming the real estate performs as projected.

Now, let's say you get up to 300 investors, you're able to increase your deal flow to two deals per year, and your average investment amount increases to $75,000.

- **300 investors x $75,000 per investment = $22,500,000**
- **2% upfront fee = $450,000**
- **1% average annual performance fee during hold period = $225,000**

Based on these metrics, if you can raise $22,500,000 in 12 months and receive a 2% upfront fee, you'd receive $450,000 in income that year and be secured in the top 1% of income earners in the U.S. Oh, and don't forget about the additional $1,125,000 you're set to receive over the next five years from the performance of the real estate.

Boom! You've made it. And this doesn't even include the other income you'd be set to receive based on the performance of the previous assets you were raising capital for.

The first time I ran these numbers, I thought I was calculating them incorrectly. It seemed too fantastic to think that such a small number of investors could create such an incredible income for a real estate entrepreneur, but this is the reality that several major players in the sector are living in right now.

Of course, there are firms that exceed this, but raising this amount of capital would be an exceptional accomplishment and would solidify your position as a high performer in the real estate sector.

Having said that, is it really that outlandish to think that you could be one of those top performers? Think about it. All it takes is 300 investors who are willing to invest $75,000 in a given year.

It's definitely feasible, although this isn't an easy feat and there are many caveats to this formula:

- Some may not invest every single year, meaning you'd need more than 300 active investors in your network.
- Recessions could cause people to stop investing in real estate (at the exact time there's the most opportunity).
- Your investments may under-perform, which would reduce your anticipated average performance compensation, the size of your investor base, the frequency at which those remaining invest, and the size of their investments (which is why it's so important to depend on the right operating partner).

But even when considering those factors, is it really that unreasonable?

Keep in mind, with only 300 out of the 12,000,000 accredited families, you're capturing .0025% of the market (when counting each accredited household as one potential investor).

These numbers are, in part, why I was so motivated to write this book, and why I decided to move forward with creating our podcast, unafraid to give away the trade secrets of the business. There are 12,000,000 accredited investor households and all you'd need is a few hundred dedicated investors to accomplish some truly remarkable things. To me, this puts everything in perspective.

CHAPTER 16

Going All-In vs. Making Excuses

I f you've followed along so far, you've probably not only learned a lot of key takeaways (and hopefully some **$2,000 Ideas**) but also bought into my perspective on how to create a streamlined structure for raising capital. However, while the systems I've outlined may make logical sense, and the strategies may even seem achievable, there might be something in the back of your head telling you that it won't be that easy. Maybe there's some lingering doubt from another time when you were similarly motivated but ultimately disheartened when it didn't turn out like you expected. In short, there could be something telling you that putting the time towards implementing these strategies simply isn't going to work for you.

Let's unpack this.

First of all, you're right: It isn't going to be easy at all. If you recall from the first few chapters, in order to be successful in the real estate sector, you'll need to be obsessed with becoming an expert. Truth be told, having a thorough understanding of the real estate space is just the baseline. In this industry, not only do you have to actually be an expert, you also have to be *perceived* as one. Luckily, your expertise can be supercharged by some of the strategies I discussed previously in this book, such as where to get educational content and how to create your own. But, yes, it's much easier said than done.

Once you start to grasp just how big the mountain that you're climbing is, it can be a bit intimidating. Plenty of people might be inclined to go from 100% motivated to completely deflated once they realize the magnitude of the journey on which they are embarking. In order to overcome this, it's important to prepare for things to go wrong and be able to meet adversity head-on, challenge after challenge.

Other than being unprepared for challenges, another major inhibitor of real estate entrepreneurial success is the tendency to compare your progress to that of others in the sector, especially if you don't have a healthy relationship with competition.

Generally speaking, I'm a very competitive person. However, I've learned to use this part of my personality as a motivating factor, as opposed to one that detracts from my forward progress.

What does this mean?

I'm significantly motivated by the success of others. Also, I don't want my competitors to do poorly, very much the opposite: I want my competitors to blow it out of the water. I just want to ensure that I do so as well. Ever since I was young, if I didn't see myself in a position to potentially be in the top tier amongst my peers (regardless of what I was focusing on), I'd find some other pursuit. This desire is actually one of the things that led me to real estate: It suited my natural strengths, which I felt gave me an advantage.

Why am I telling you this? Despite having this type of relationship with competition, which I recognize not everyone has, any time I see someone who's significantly more successful than I am, my mind immediately wants to come up with excuses as to why their success doesn't apply to me. Rather than looking for ways I can learn from them, I tend to initially look for a cop out.

I'll give you an example. We recently contracted a joint venture (JV) partnership with one of our operating partners in which we'll be investing $15,000,000 over the coming years. During negotiations with the operating partner, their principal mentioned that they have another JV partner who just signed a similar agreement, only the other firm, we'll call them ABC Investments, will be investing $35,000,000 over the same time period.

Just knowing that the other firm was capable of investing more than double what we had the capacity to stung a bit. So, what did I do? Reverted to my typical pattern: I started researching the firm (*What is its market advantage? When was it established? Who are the main people involved?*) hoping to find several glaring reasons why it had a massive head start on me, so I could justify the $20,000,000 discrepancy in capital commitment for our respective JV partnerships.

If there's one distinction I can usually rely on, it's that most of the players in the real estate sector are a lot older than me.

Real estate is typically thought of as a "get rich slow" game, so time is usually on my side. If you're a young up-and-comer in the real estate sector, you know what I'm talking about. Much to my chagrin, I found out the worst-case scenario. Not only was the company founded after mine, its principal is a few months younger than me.

At this point, I felt the self-defense mechanism kicked in. My mind didn't want to face the fact that he's been able to accomplish some unbelievably remarkable things in his career, despite only being in the business for less than 10 years.

Not long into my investigation, I discovered a cop-out lifeline. As it turns out, the principal of this firm is a graduate of Harvard and Harvard Business School, the son of a real estate magnate, and, what's more, extremely well-connected politically.

My mind reveled in this new information.

There it is! An easy out. The guy is probably a genius, and even if he isn't, he probably had enough help from his dad or political associates to make up for any of his weaknesses.

No need to dig any further. No need to contemplate how hard he worked to sustain an Ivy League education. No need to consider the fact that he has built an investor base of thousands of investors and has been able to consistently deliver for them for years. No need to consider the fact that, while his father may have been in the real estate business many years ago, his father certainly didn't source the relationship with this particular operating partner, who wasn't even in business when his father was active in the sector. No need to consider the fact that his firm has dozens of employees whom he somehow inspires every day to come to work, look up to him, and trust him with their livelihood.

As a competitive person, and a human being in general, I recognize that my mind is naturally going to attempt this kind of mental gymnastics in order to avoid facing the reality of the situation.

Yes, it's probably true that the principal of ABC Investments was born with a lot of advantages that helped him ramp up from 0 to 60 much faster than he would have otherwise. However, it's also the case that the success of his firm, which has been pronounced for years, is a result of incredibly hard work, intuition, dedication, and a perfect combination of the KMIs I discussed previously.

I'm sharing this with you because you might be doing the exact same thing right now. Maybe you're dreaming of the day when you can raise $10,000,000 for an offering, but you're simultaneously coming up with all the reasons why the systems and strategies outlined in this book have worked for me but won't work for you.

Don't worry, that's completely natural and will likely happen intermittently for the rest of your life. It happens to me. It happens to the people I look up to. And it happens to the people they look up to as well. Don't beat yourself up about it.

However, part of what I want you to get out of this chapter is this: **stop being intimidated by other people's success and start being inspired by it.**

If you find out that one of your competitors has raised $100,000,000, that's incredibly good news. It means if they can do it, it's likely that you can do it too. The more people that you know who've accomplished something incredible in business, the clearer it should become that remarkable things are possible. **Once you start to see other's success as inspiration, you start to become infinitely motivated rather than perpetually discouraged.**

Like I mentioned, the strategies laid out in this book aren't going to be easy to implement at the ultra-high level. It's going to take blood, sweat, and years. However, if financial wealth and personal freedom are your main goals, and you're looking for a high degree of certainty in terms of accomplishing these goals, the strategies outlined in this book are the most direct route I've found to get there.

In fact, I know a company managed by relatively young key principals that went from $0 to $1,000,000,000 of assets under management in less than 10 years. I know of another company run by an equally young team that went from $0 to $500,000,000 in less than three years. Rather than trying to check the background of the key principals in an effort to justify why Asym didn't grow at those rates, I use them as inspiration. I rub elbows with these firms, learn from their principals, host them as guests on my podcasts and at my conference, and implement the strategies they share with me.

RESULTS OF GOING ALL-IN

Prior to getting into the real estate sector, I was only considered a "hard worker" by the people who knew me extremely well. I was a B-student who discovered early on that I was unmotivated by working for someone else. In short, I wasn't a genius who thrived in academia or the typical work environment. This doesn't bother me at all now, but it was pretty scary when I was still in school or working at jobs where I clearly wasn't really bringing anything special to the table. I figured that's what the rest of my life would be like. I'm sure many of you reading this can relate.

However, once I realized my path and as soon as I started to gain some momentum in the real estate sector, I went all-in. Going all-in isn't something that takes natural talent or something you're born with; it's simply a measure of the amount of action you're willing to take on a consistent basis, regardless of your starting point, to achieve your goals. It's the real X factor that differentiates high performers from everyone else.

What does that mean? It means constant dedication and motivation. It means staying focused and not wavering when things don't go your way. It means devoting yourself to becoming a master in your field then sticking with it through thick and thin.

If you commit to implementing the strategies outlined in this book, the results will speak for themselves.

With that in mind, I want to share with you an email I received from an investor after I'd implemented the steps outlined in this book:

Hello Hunter,

I found out about Asym Capital yesterday, and today I learned about the fund that's currently available. I'm an accredited investor and interested in participating in this fund but noticed the funding date is very soon. I'd like to send in my signed interest form and follow up with a letter from my CPA and fund after that, but I wanted to send you this message through the portal now, given that the cutoff is soon. FYI, I've been a real estate investor of single-family properties in the Sun Belt since the early 2000s, have a small number of properties in Houston, Texas and currently work for Amazon in Seattle, Washington. I found out about you from your interview on Cashflow Ninja's podcast yesterday and listened to several of your podcasts this morning.

First and foremost, I want to thank M.C Laubscher, the host of the *Cashflow Ninja Podcast* for asking for me to be a guest on the show. If you want to listen to the interview that I gave, which resulted in this inquiry, please visit www.cashflowninja.com/462-hunter-thompson.

The investor ended up investing $50,000 within 24 hours of finding out about our firm. This happened because once they became aware of who we are and visited our website, they immediately discovered a robust infrastructure that would educate them on our way of investing. In a very short amount of time and with little interaction, we were able to establish enough credibility for them to entrust us with their hard-earned capital.

As made clear in their email, the investor was already familiar with real estate and had enough knowledge to quickly conduct due diligence on our specific offering. This might not always be the case, but it sure feels good when investors come in eager to invest based on the educational content you've put out.

I also recently received a separate email from a different investor right after they had invested with us for the first time.

I'd just sent them a thank-you email, and this was their response. Note that the infrastructure we've created was as helpful in this circumstance, but in a different way:

Hunter,

Being rather new to investing in real estate assets, I realize I'm placing significant trust in your aptitudes within this sector. Having said that, I've been a diligent student of the podcast since hearing your interview with Tom Woods a couple years ago. It's apparent to me you're an effective team leader with the integrity of the team at the core of your business pursuits. I'm investing with you because I have confidence in not only your acumen with real estate, but in your ability to effectively network with what likely are some of the best operators in the business. Last, but certainly not least, I appreciate the integrity I'm observing infused with humility, a virtue without equal.

Kind regards and I look forward to sharing this opportunity with you.

Of course, I'd like to thank Tom Woods for having me on his show as well. If you want to check out that interview, please visit ww.tomwoods.com/ep-917-the-truth-about-the-real-estate-market-and-what-regular-people-should-do.

There are several reasons I wanted to include this email here. First of all, this personal communication is from an investor who was on our email list for almost three years before ever making an investment. If we didn't have a system for consistent follow up, I certainly would've given up courting them as an investor, another reminder of the importance of creating an automated lead-nurture system. When it comes to investors who aren't ready to move forward immediately upon introduction, you need to consistently provide them with new, enriching content so they can take their time getting acquainted with a topic that they might not already be familiar with.

Another aspect I love about this email is that it shows how much the investor knows about me and our company culture solely from the content we've created, and that content has shown us to be a high-integrity group worthy of their trust. As I mentioned previously, the podcast medium is the most intimate form of educational content because you're literally plugged into people's ears. Because they're able to do multiple things while listening to podcasts, they can be tuned in for much longer without interruption, which also heightens their ability to digest the content, as opposed to having several 10-minute attention spurts.

Lastly, as a nice bonus, this investor likely believed that my thank-you email was the final correspondence they'd receive until the initial quarterly report. However, what they didn't know is they'd soon receive a personalized thank-you note signed by me as well. In the thank-you note, I made a direct mention of the exact things the investor alluded to in their email, specifically related to my understanding that their investment with our firm represented a significant amount of trust.

These emails are proof that the system is working and the dedication that it took to create the infrastructure was well worth it. Receiving these types of emails really does make my day, and this is something that happens on a very regular basis.

In fact, virtually every single one of our investors has a very similar story as to how they came to invest with our firm, whether or not they send an email like this. Trust me, I know. I ask each of them when we speak for the first time on our introductory call, and the vast majority were either drawn in by educational content or were referred by a previous investor who originally found us via our online presence.

Closing

I wrote this book because I want to play an influential role in others' success in the real estate sector. I was extremely fortunate to have met the people I did early on in my career, and without them, I certainly wouldn't be where I am today. The importance of those early relationships compelled me to create a similar opportunity for those in the same position I was when I got started. In short, I want others to benefit from the lessons I've learned through the years, so they can supercharge their learning curve and get results as soon as possible.

While I've enjoyed the personal benefits of success, nothing brings me more happiness than helping create that success for other people. It brings me great pleasure to receive emails from graduates of the CFC Mentorship Program about their big wins, as well as the success stories of our *Cash Flow Connections Real Estate Podcast* listeners. It's the best part of my job and propels me even further forward in my career.

This is my blueprint for raising significant capital for real estate. It's the most streamlined and concise approach that I've found to creating wealth, while enjoying a high degree of personal freedom along the way.

However, just understanding the concepts in this short book isn't going to be enough. You have to take consistent and unwavering action to get the results you're looking for. The steps have been laid out clearly. The only question is whether or not you will take them.

If you've made it this far, I'm confident you're the caliber of person who can take this content and get results akin to the success stories I've outlined throughout these chapters. So, what's the difference between the passive reader who has enjoyed the book but isn't going to implement the strategies and the person who will read this book and immediately hit the ground running? Simple.

The key difference is the exact same five KMIs I outlined in Chapter 3, about how to attract a successful mentor:

1. **Sense of urgency to accomplish your goals**
2. **High speed of execution and implementation**
3. **Attention to detail and high demand for excellence**
4. **Obsession with growth**
5. **Curiosity about new topics and a desire for expertise**

It's one thing to outwardly project these qualities to others for the purposes of attracting a mentor, it's an entirely different thing to actually anchor your everyday actions in these traits. If you're able to authentically embody these five characteristics, you'll see results faster than you previously thought possible.

If some don't come naturally to you, no need to worry. Just recognize that all of these traits are critical to your success and continue to focus on bringing all of your KMIs up to elite levels by consistently honing your skills. It's a never-ending process.

As discussed in Chapter 3, the reason high performers look for these attributes in young up-and-comers is these are characteristics of virtually all successful people. Regardless of how far along you are in your career, if you embody these attributes, it'll be clear to anyone that you're well on your way towards excellence. Your momentum will be magnetic, and everyone around you will feel it and want to help you along your way.

If you break it down, what I'm saying is this: Be best-in-class at something that's highly complicated and competitive. I know that sounds a bit intimidating, but there's no reason you can't do it by implementing the steps I've laid out in these pages. If you're intimidated, that just means you're onto something monumental. I'm telling you right now: Solely understanding the concepts in this book is a great start, but if you integrate the educational content in this book with the five KMIs listed above, you're going to be on the fast track to abundant wealth and personal freedom.

I can't wait to hear how your capital raising journey goes.

Email me at hunter@raisingcapitalforrealestate.com when you've raised your first $1,000,000, $5,000,000, and $10,000,000.